Key Concepts 2

- **Listening, Note Taking, and**
- **Speaking Across the Disciplines**

Key Concepts 2

Listening, Note Taking, and Speaking Across the Disciplines

Elena Vestri Solomon

Hillsborough Community College

John L. Shelley

Additional information and activities can be found at the
Key Concepts 2 website: *elt.heinle.com/keyconcepts*.

HEINLE
CENGAGE Learning

Australia • Brazil • Japan • Korea • Mexico • Singapore • Spain • United Kingdom • United States

Key Concepts 2: Listening, Note Taking, and Speaking Across the Disciplines
Elena Vestri Solomon / John L. Shelley

Publisher: Patricia A. Coryell

Senior Development Editor: Kathy Sands-Boehmer

Development Editor: Kathleen M. Smith

Editorial Assistant: Evangeline Bermas

Project Editor: Kerry Doyle

Executive Marketing Manager: Annamarie Rice

Marketing Assistant: Andrew Whitacre

Compositor: Publishing Services

Cover Image: © David Zaitz/Photonica

Library of Congress Number: 2005930757

ISBN-13: 978-0-618-38241-5

ISBN-10: 0-618-38241-0

Heinle
25 Thomson Place
Boston, MA 02210
USA

Cengage Learning is a leading provider of customized learning solutions with office locations around the globe, including Singapore, the United Kingdom, Australia, Mexico, Brazil and Japan. Locate our local office at: **international.cengage.com/region**

Cengage Learning products are represented in Canada by Nelson Education, Ltd.

Visit Heinle online at **elt.heinle.com**
Visit our corporate website at **cengage.com**

Photo Credits: Page 14 © MedioImages/SuperStock; Page 37 © Royalty-Free/CORBIS; Page 57 © William Whitehurst/CORBIS; Page 89 Courtesy of the Berkshire Museum, Pittsfield, Massachusetts; Page 106 © James L. Amos/CORBIS; Page 109 © Bettmann/CORBIS.

Printed in Canada
5 6 7 8 9 10   12 11 10 09 08

Contents

Key Concepts 2: Listening, Note Taking, and Speaking Across the Disciplines

Additional activities and information can be found at the
Key Concepts 2 website: *elt.heinle.com/keyconcepts.*

● Key Concepts 2 Skills Overview

Listening for ...				Speaking
Chapter	Pronunciation	Note Taking	Discourse Markers and Commonly Used Expressions*	
1		• outlining • word maps • Cornell method • key word method • paragraph method		survey
2	Stress and Pitch Patterns	outlining	Discourse Markers and Commonly Used Expressions	summary
3	Stress for Meaning	choice	Discourse Markers and Commonly Used Expressions	extemporaneous speech
4	Pauses	choice	Discourse Markers	interview
5	Modals *can* and *can't*	choice	Discourse Markers	explain a visual
6	Vowel and Syllable Length in Stress and Pitch	choice	Discourse Markers and Commonly Used Expressions	debate
7	Modal Auxiliaries	choice	Discourse Markers	group presentation

*See Appendix 2 for a comprehensive list of Discourse Markers and Commonly Used Expressions.

Introduction

Key Concepts 2, the second in a two-volume series, is a high-intermediate text that focuses on the academic skills of listening, note taking, vocabulary building, and speaking. However, the most important element of the *Key Concepts* series is the subject matter itself, both in the text and on the accompanying audio program. The themes of these texts mirror the academic curricula that meet the general education requirements at most U.S. community colleges and universities. *Key Concepts* allows students to improve their academic preparation by giving them an understanding of the main concepts and lecture points they will encounter in their higher education. The chapters of *Key Concepts 2* include topics from the following college majors:

- Social Sciences: Cultural Anthropology
- Business: Business Ethics
- Language Arts: English Literature
- Mathematics: Applied Mathematics
- History: American History
- Physical Sciences: Physics

For many ESL students, the term "academic English" typically brings to mind grammar, writing, and reading texts. While these are, of course, important, we believe that far too few texts foster improvement of academic communication and listening, which should be learned in conjunction with these skills. In contrast, *Key Concepts* prepares students for the many academic tasks they will face in higher education by providing an active listening/speaking component throughout the text. This material includes the understanding of key points and broad themes of the various disciplines, listening for details, note-taking strategies, understanding discourse markers, academic vocabulary practice, and speaking tasks. The listening skills exercises, group-work, and speaking activities are keyed to the particular themes of each chapter, thus offering the student a consistent and unified approach to learning the material.

In addition to content-specific vocabulary, each chapter of *Key Concepts* introduces and offers extensive practice with twenty vocabulary items from Averil Coxhead's Academic Word List. These words are the most frequently used vocabulary in college-level texts. *Key Concepts 1* contains the first 120 lexical items on the list and *Key Concepts 2* continues with the next 120. Each chapter includes definitions and vocabulary exercises that afford students ample practice with these words. One salient feature of *Key Concepts 2* is its attention to word forms for building vocabulary. Along with learning the AWL words, the students are given the tools to discern their forms and usage in various parts of speech.

Text Organization

The skills practiced in *Key Concepts* can be broken down into the following:

- 50% listening: main ideas, details, inference, note-taking
- 30% vocabulary building: high-frequency vocabulary, content-based vocabulary, discourse markers (transitions), idiomatic expressions
- 20% speaking: recycling vocabulary and content, negotiating meaning, formal presentation skills, group problem-solving

The text is divided into seven chapters and seven appendixes.

Chapter Listening and Speaking Components

Listening 1: Short Conversations

The first listening task includes the following activities: getting ready to listen with brainstorming and discussion, listening for meaning and inference, and listening to authentic dialogues typical to a campus environment.

Listening 2: Mini-Lecture

To prepare for the second listening task, students are introduced to ten vocabulary items from the Academic Word List, which they will practice in different exercise formats. This practice is followed by a mini-lecture, for which the students use one of six distinct note-taking strategies presented in Chapter 1. They then use their notes to answer comprehension questions about the lecture.

Listening 3: Pronunciation

These discrete listening activities exploit a variety of points in the short conversations, mini-lectures, and extended lectures and ask students to concentrate on specific pronunciation elements or vocabulary items.

Listening 4: Extended Lecture

To prepare students for the extended lecture portion of the chapter, discourse marker and commonly used phrases exercises are included. Students work with the meanings and usage of these items to better prepare themselves for their occurrence in the extended lecture. The remaining complement of vocabulary from the Academic Word List for the unit is presented in this section. Note taking is again reinforced. Comprehension questions and a critical thinking activity follow.

Speaking

Each chapter ends with students practicing different speaking strategies. They are conducting surveys, interviewing, extemporaneous speaking, debating, presenting as a group, summarizing, and explaining a visual.

Each chapter includes a final activity related to the speaking strategy. Time permitting, instructors may choose to have all the students participate in this expansion activity or assign it as extra credit.

Online Resources

Additional Web Activities for Students at elt.heinle.com/keyconcepts

The *Key Concepts* series also offers additional activities using audio recordings. These listening activities are connected to the disciplines presented in each chapter. Students can listen to the lecture, then practice note taking, listening, and vocabulary by logging on to the Heinle website at *elt.heinle.com/keyconcepts*.

Instructor Manual and Answer Key

The instructor manual and answer key for the *Key Concepts* series are available on the Heinle website at *elt.heinle.com/keyconcepts*.

Assessment

Every chapter contains additional lectures that are available online for instructors to download as assessment tools. Comprehensive tests accompany the lectures. These tests include areas for students to take notes, comprehension questions, and vocabulary items from the Academic Word List. Instructors may use the audio programs or choose to deliver the lectures themselves. For these instructors, note cards can be downloaded, printed, and used to present the lecture "naturally" to the class. Accompanying comprehension tests can be downloaded by instructors and given to students. The instructor site also contains a variety of web activities for instructors to give to students.

Acknowledgments

We would like to thank the many faculty members of Hillsborough Community College who gave tireless input and feedback on the academic requirements of their disciplines. Their expertise was paramount to the creation of the content-driven chapters. We express equal gratitude to our ESL colleagues who shared their ideas and insights on the value of oral communication and methods of achieving academic success in listening and speaking.

Our editors, Susan Maguire and Kathy Sands-Boehmer, gave us guidance and support throughout the entire process, to which we are extremely grateful. We couldn't have asked for a better development editor, Kathleen Smith, whose ideas, feedback, and input have made our work that much better.

Our gratitude also goes out to the many reviewers who commented on our manuscripts, offering advice and suggestions that helped create our final product. They are:

Anne Bachman, *Clackamas Community College*

Richard Cervin, *Sacramento City College*

Maggie Discont, *West Hills College*

Mark Ende, *Onondaga Community College*

Carolyn Ho, *Cy Fair College*

Michael Khirallah, *Oakland Community College*

Carole Marquis, *Santa Fe Community College*

Dan Smolens, *Roxbury Community College*

Kent Trickel, *Westchester Community College*

Last, our thanks go out to our many ESL and EFL students who, over the years, have given us the drive to continue learning, evaluating, and improving.

Elena Vestri Solomon
John L. Shelley

CITY COLLEGE
Office of the Registrar
OFFICIAL TRANSCRIPT

Student No: 789-56-1234   Date of Birth: 10 JAN 1985

Record of: JOE RODRIGUEZ
Major: LIBERAL ARTS
Year of Graduation: 2008

SUBJECT	NO.	COURSE TITLE	CREDITS	GRADE
FALL 2005			3	A
ENGL	1101	Freshman English	3	A
BIOL	1201	Intro to Biology	3	B
FREN	1001	Intro to French	3	B
PHIL	1500	Philosophy	3	A
MATH	0900	Applied Mathematics	3	B
GOVT	1735	Early American Government	3	

Earned Credits: 18.00
GPA Points: 63.00
Current GPA: 3.50

1 Student Success

One of the most influential times in a person's life is his or her educational experience. Many people want to have great careers, an abundance of wealth, and respect from their peers. One of the most rewarding ways of attaining these goals is a solid education.

Key Concepts 2 will aid you in your educational goals. By studying the information presented, you will arm yourself with some of the necessary skills to be successful in college.

This short chapter will help you understand some **key concepts** of success in college such as

• time management

• note-taking basics

• vocabulary development

It will also prepare you for many of the activities that follow in the text.

ACTIVITY 1 *Check Your Schedule*

How well do you manage your time? Look at the following schedule and spend at least 10 minutes filling it out. Include your work, school, travel, and study time. Don't forget to write in your leisure time!

	Monday	Tuesday	Wednesday	Thursday	Friday	Saturday	Sunday
6:00							
7:00							
8:00							
9:00							
10:00							
11:00							
12:00							
1:00							
2:00							
3:00							
4:00							
5:00–8:00							
8:00–11:00							

Now exchange schedules with a classmate. How many hours of study time does your partner use? Is there anything that your classmate is doing that you consider an ineffective use of time?

Listen and Take Notes

ACTIVITY ❷

Listen to Mini-Lecture 1: Managing Time in College

Listen to a short lecture on the importance of time management. As you listen the first time, write down the most important information you hear. Then listen a second time and fill in any information that you might have missed. When you are finished, compare your notes with those of a classmate.

LISTENING 2 ● **Note-Taking Methods**

There are many ways to take notes when you listen to a lecture. Some students take notes using abbreviations (see Appendix 5 for more information). Others like to use a standard outline form with letters and numbers. Still others like to take notes in paragraph form.

There is no one correct way to take notes. The method you choose should be one that you are comfortable with. Study the various note-taking methods in this section. They all use the mini-lecture Managing Time in College as an example. Which method is closest to the way you usually take notes?

Outline Method

One method of recording is using an outline. Because teachers who prepare lectures well tend to speak in organized and logical patterns, it can be easy for students to use the outline format when they take notes. The outline form is similar to what students use when they prepare to write an academic paper.

I. Introduction
   A. Students and Time Management
      1. Students think they're good
      2. FALSE!
         a. Cramming for tests
         b. Up all night
         c. Homework in class
   B. Time as resource
      1. Not renewable — unlike money
      2. When finished, can't get it back

II. Steps
   A. Observe how you use time
      1. Time chart
      2. Fill it out
      3. Group activities
         a. Sleep
         b. Class
         c. Study
         d. Work
         e. Meals
         f. Entertainment
   B. Strategy
      1. Make a list
      2. Use ABC method
         a. A - most important
         b. B - less important
         c. C - small jobs
      3. Cross off things as you do them
         a. Evaluate list at end of day
         b. Write new list for tomorrow
         c. Think about moving tasks from one list to another

Word Maps

Another way of taking good notes is to use word maps. A word map consists of connected circles, each with important information in it. These circles connect ideas with lines from one circle to another. The large central circles contain main ideas, and the outer connected circles contain supporting or related details. The information usually starts from the center and moves outward as the information gets more specific.

The Cornell Method

Many students use the Cornell Method to take notes. In this method you divide the paper into two columns. You record main points in the left column and related or supporting details in the right column.

Student time management	Most students NOT good cram for tests up all night do homework in class
Time	Resource: not renewable
Observe use of time	use a time chart put activities in groups (class, work, etc)
Time Strategy	make a list
ABC method	A - most important B - less important C - small jobs
Final steps	Cross things off evaluate list at end of day write new list for tomorrow move tasks from one list to another

Key Concepts 2: Listening, Note Taking, and Speaking Across the Disciplines

Key Word Method

When you listen to a lecture, there will always be important vocabulary that you need to recognize and understand. Key words or phrases contain the essence of communication. They include specific content words (technical words that are related to the subject), names, numbers, equations, and words of degree, such as *better, most, least*, etc.

Sometimes you can take effective notes just by writing down key words along with a few explanatory words. Notice that in this method, you usually don't record as many details.

STUDENTS BAD WITH TIME

TIME AS RESOURCE

OBSERVATION — time chart

ABC — most important → least

EVALUATION

Paragraph Method

Some students' preferred way of taking notes is to write the information in paragraph form. Writing notes as paragraphs is different from creating your own original paragraph. Paragraphs you write in note taking are shorter, and they don't include every word that the speaker is saying. However, they should include any key words you hear. It's easier to use paragraphs in note taking if the teacher is speaking slowly.

Students come to college + think — very good at managing time. That's not true. They cram, up all night, + finish homework in class. Time = nonrenewable. If no money, you go to ATM. Time is different. When it's gone, that's it.

The first thing is observe how you use time. Get a chart. Fill in every day for a week. Evaluate it. Make groups. Sleep, class, study, work, ... Do you see where you waste time? Find a strategy. The most popular is a daily list of "things to do," like ABC method. Separate into three categories: A = most important, like classroom assignments. B list is things that are important, but not like A. Your final is C list, easy jobs with no time limit.

Cross it off your list when finish. Look at your list every day. Rewrite what's not finished. Move C list to A/B lists.

Listen and Take Notes

ACTIVITY **3**

Listen to Mini-Lecture 2: Note-Taking Strategies

Listen to the short lecture about being a good note taker. Then take notes on the information using one of the note-taking strategies you just studied.

Note-Taking Method: _____

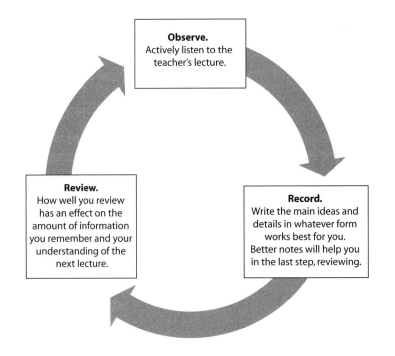

Observe.
Actively listen to the teacher's lecture.

Record.
Write the main ideas and details in whatever form works best for you. Better notes will help you in the last step, reviewing.

Review.
How well you review has an effect on the amount of information you remember and your understanding of the next lecture.

Compare your notes with those of your classmates.

Vocabulary Development

Having a varied vocabulary is an integral part of being a good student. One way of accomplishing this is to learn various word forms of vocabulary you already know. Word forms are simply the different parts of speech of a word. Let's review the different parts of speech.

Nouns — people, places, things, concepts, and feelings

Verbs — actions or states of mind or being

Adjectives — words that describe nouns

Adverbs — words that describe verbs, adjectives, and other adverbs. They tell how, when, frequency, or intensity.

ACTIVITY ❹   ***Identify Parts of Speech***

A. Read this sentence and answer questions about the underlined words.

Some <u>students</u> <u>learn</u> <u>note-taking</u> <u>skills</u> <u>very</u> <u>quickly</u>.

1. Which word tells you who learns? _____
   What part of speech is it? _____
2. Which word tells you what students do? _____
   What part of speech is it? _____
3. Which word tells you how they do it? _____
   What part of speech is it? _____
4. Which word tells you how quickly they do it? _____
   What part of speech is it? _____
5. Which word tells you what they learn? _____
   What part of speech is it? _____
6. Which word tells you what kind of skills they learn? _____
   What part of speech is it? _____

B. Look at the underlined words in each sentence. Write **N** (noun), **V** (verb), **Adj** (adjective), or **Adv** (adverb) above each word.

1. Those students are taking a very difficult test.

2. Some teachers believe that good note-taking skills seriously impact a student's success in the classroom.

3. That English course is almost completely full.

4. Many international students work diligently at part-time jobs.

In future chapters, you will learn important rules for making different forms of many words, both rules you already know and new rules.

ACTIVITY **5**

Work with Word Forms

Complete each sentence with the appropriate form of the word in parentheses. Then circle the part of speech that the word is used as in the sentence. The first one is done for you.

1. (patience) Joann wasn't very _patient_ today in class. In fact, I could hear her muttering during Dr. Smith's lecture.

   Part of speech: noun   verb   (adjective)   adverb

2. (observe) Did you _____ how nervous Lenny was during his oral presentation? He was sweating!

   Part of speech: noun   verb   adjective   adverb

3. (casual) You need to pay attention in this English class. You can't _____ walk in 5 minutes after class has started and expect to understand what's going on.

   Part of speech: noun   verb   adjective   adverb

4. (lecture) There will be a new _____ next week. I think he's from India.

   Part of speech: noun   verb   adjective   adverb

5. (moderation) Janice is going to _____ our debate tomorrow. She's very good at it.

   Part of speech: noun   verb   adjective   adverb

6. (rely) The computer lab isn't very _____. I've already lost three papers on the hard drive.

   Part of speech: noun   verb   adjective   adverb

You will learn more about creating word forms in the upcoming chapters.

Phrasal Verbs

A phrasal verb, also called a two-part verb, is a combination verb + preposition. These two- or three-part elements, when put together as a phrasal verb, generally have a different meaning than the same words used individually. Study these examples.

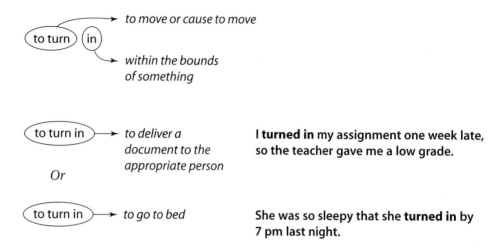

I **turned in** my assignment one week late, so the teacher gave me a low grade.

She was so sleepy that she **turned in** by 7 pm last night.

Phrasal verbs are very common, especially in spoken language. English speakers are more likely to say, "Did you **find out** when the final exam will be?" than "Did you discover when the final exam will be?"

You will have ample practice with phrasal verbs in *Key Concepts 2*. For more information on phrasal verbs, see Appendix 3 on p. 132.

ACTIVITY **6**

Work with Phrasal Verbs

Read the following sentences. If you think that the underlined phrase is a phrasal verb, circle *phrasal verb* and try to guess the meaning. If the underlined phrase is NOT a phrasal verb, circle *literal meaning* and leave the space blank.

1. When we <u>looked up</u>, we saw that class was almost over and we wouldn't have time to finish the exam.

   literal meaning   phrasal verb (*meaning:* _____)

2. The teacher didn't bring her umbrella to school yesterday; she didn't <u>count on</u> that huge thunderstorm.

   literal meaning   phrasal verb (*meaning:* _____)

3. A lot of roommates don't <u>hit it off</u> for the first few weeks after moving into the same dorm room.

   literal meaning   phrasal verb (*meaning:* _____)

4. Sherry <u>went overboard</u> when she saw that her expensive ring had fallen off the boat into the ocean.

   literal meaning   phrasal verb (*meaning:* _____)

5. They're never going to <u>iron out</u> their problems; they're just too different.

    literal meaning   phrasal verb (*meaning:* _____)

6. No one <u>looks up to</u> the dean of student services because he's never around to help out.

    literal meaning   phrasal verb (*meaning:* _____)

SPEAKING   • Surveying

ACTIVITY 7

Conduct Surveys about Student Success

In this activity, you will ask and answer survey questions about each other's time management and note-taking skills.

Task

Your teacher will put you into two groups.

In your group, brainstorm at least five questions related to the topic that is given to you. After you write the questions, choose one person to conduct the survey. This person is also responsible for recording the other group's individual answers.

When both groups are finished creating the survey questions, have the survey conductors switch groups to gather the information. Use a data sheet like the one below.

Q1: _____
  A: _____
  A: _____
  A: _____
  A: _____
etc.
Q2: _____
  A: _____
etc.

Group 1 Topic: Time management skills (You may want to refer to page 3 in this chapter and listen to the mini-lecture on Managing Time in College for ideas for questions.)

Group 2 Topic: Note-taking skills (You may want to refer to pages 3–8 in this chapter and listen to the mini-lecture on Note-Taking Strategies for ideas for questions.)

Tips for Asking and Answering Survey Questions

1. Avoid writing YES or NO questions (Do you study in the library?) These types of questions limit the information you receive. Instead, ask open-ended questions beginning with *what, who, where, why,* and *how* (Where do you study, and what do you like about that place?). These questions will encourage the person you are surveying to give longer answers.

2. If the person does not understand the question, restate it another way or give an example of how you would answer the question. Likewise, if you don't understand the answer, ask for a clarification.

3. Be careful of your tone of voice. Do not make judgments about the person being interviewed. A question such as "Do you think you would get better grades if you studied more?" is not appropriate.

4. If you are asking the questions, be sure to write down all the information that is being presented to you. Without this information, you cannot summarize the group's ideas.

NOTE: Refer to Appendix 6 on pp. 141–143 for more information on interactive speaking strategies.

ACTIVITY **8**

Conduct Another Survey

Now that you know how to conduct a survey, try creating one for another class. Choose a topic that you are interested in getting more information about. Write five to ten questions about the topic and invite your classmates to participate. After you compile your answers, share them with the group and your instructor.

For more activities and information, go to the *Key Concepts* 2 website at *elt.heinle.com/keyconcepts*.

2 From the Social Sciences: Cultural Anthropology

ANT-2100
Introduction to Cultural Anthropology (3)
This course is an introduction to the study of social and cultural behavior—the beliefs, customs, values, languages, and goals of human societies. It examines both the shared characteristics of all human social groups and the differences determined by culture. A variety of cultures will be compared and contrasted.

Anthropology is a broad field of study divided into two categories, physical anthropology and cultural anthropology. Physical anthropology studies human evolution. Cultural anthropology examines and compares behavior in present and past societies, the development of civilization, and the meaning and uses of language. Read the description on the left of a required course for all cultural anthropology majors.

Now find a course description for an introductory anthropology course from your community college or university catalog. What similarities do the two courses have? What are the differences?

This chapter will help you understand some **key concepts** of anthropology, such as

• some universal similarities among human beings

• ways in which humans interact socially

• the community structures and rules of behavior all societies share

• categories of religious and supernatural beliefs in the world

You will also practice some academic skills for success.

Get Ready to Listen

ACTIVITY **1**

Brainstorming and Discussion

A. We can divide the needs of human beings into two categories — physical and psychological/social. What needs do you think all people must satisfy in order to live happily? Put your ideas in order of importance under the two headings in the chart. Some may be equally important. Next, get into groups to discuss similarities and differences in your charts.

PHYSICAL NEEDS	PSYCHOLOGICAL NEEDS
food	love

B. Now read the following passage on the hierarchy of human needs developed by Abraham Maslow. Which ideas did your group have in Part A that Maslow includes in his list? Did you have ideas that Maslow didn't include?

A hierarchy is a system that puts things in order of their importance. The psychologist Abraham Maslow developed a list of what he called the hierarchy of human needs, needs that all people must satisfy to lead successful lives. The first and most basic of Maslow's needs in this hierarchy are the physical ones such as air, water, food, sleep, and sex. Next are safety needs, which include a home and freedom from pain and fear. After these basic needs are emotional needs. Maslow said that love is one and feeling wanted is another. People need to feel that other people care about them. Love and feeling wanted are related to another need in Maslow's hierarchy — the need for *esteem*, both in what people think about themselves and what others think about them. The last need in Maslow's hierarchy is *self-actualization*. Maslow believed that if all these other needs are satisfied, then a person can reach his/her true potential as a human being.

> **esteem** — favorable regard
> **self-actualization** — the ability to use all the abilities one has for the most possible benefit

Now cover the Maslow lecture. Use one of the note-taking methods you learned in Chapter 1 to write about what you read. What can you remember? Use these cues to divide the information into its major parts:

- Maslow's Hierarchy of Needs (give definition)
- Physical Needs (5)
- Safety Needs (3)
- Emotional Needs (4)

Expressions with "Time"

Many expressions in English use the word "time" to explain a particular situation or the frequency of something. Look at the following sentence.

I have told her time after time.

What do you think the phrase *time after time* means?
Now look at the sentence again with some words added.

I have told her time after time to stop calling me so late, but she still does it.

From the context — the situation in which the expression is used — you can guess that *time after time* means that the speaker has told her many times not to call so late.
Now look at this sentence:

She took time off.

Do you know what *time off* means? Look at the phrase again in a longer sentence.

She took time off from her job after she had the baby. She'll come back to work next month.

We see from this context that *time off* means a period of time when a person leaves a job.

Listen and Respond

Listen to Conversations

Now listen to the short conversations and circle the answers that give the meaning for the time expressions you hear.

1. "For the time being" means:
   a. for now
   b. at the right moment
   c. in the future
   d. next week

2. In this conversation, "just in time" means:
   a. at some point before the library closed
   b. only then
   c. just before the library closed
   d. at the right moment

3. "Out of time" means:
   a. there is no more time
   b. there is a little time
   c. take more time
   d. take time out

4. "Take your time" means:
   a. hurry
   b. don't hurry
   c. wait until it is your turn
   d. start whenever you want to

5. "At times" means:
   a. always
   b. never
   c. occasionally
   d. often

6. "On time" means:
   a. earlier than expected
   b. later than expected
   c. sooner or later
   d. when expected

7. "From time to time" means:
   a. at a fixed moment
   b. on lots of occasions
   c. almost never
   d. occasionally

8. In this conversation, "one at a time" means:
   a. later
   b. just once
   c. they shouldn't both speak at the same time
   d. frequently

9. "Time will tell" means:
   a. it's too late to know
   b. this isn't the right moment
   c. we'll know in the future
   d. the answer will never be known

10. In this conversation, "overtime" means:
    a. more than the usual amount of time
    b. past the time when something is due
    c. paying for extra time
    d. after a while

Work with Time Words

The time words in the box are from the conversations you just heard. Use them to complete the sentences below. The first one is done for you.

for the time being	just in time	at times	out of time
take your time	from time to time	one at a time	
time will tell	~~overtime~~	on time	

1. having to spend two hours extra every day this week at my job.

   "I've been working two hours _overtime_ every day this week at my job."

2. people getting on a bus all at once

   "Please everybody, _____."

3. not knowing if your medical operation will be successful

   "It will probably be okay, but only _____."

4. waiting for the train

   "I hope it comes _____."

5. keeping in touch with old friends from high school

   "I try to call them _____."

6. a teacher sees a student making mistakes because he is going too quickly

   "Please, _____."

7. waiting outside the library until it opens

   "I'll just read the newspaper _____."

8. a teacher is saying that there is no more time for students to do the test

   "I'm sorry, but you are _____."

9. getting to the movie theater moments before the movie starts

   "We got here _____."

10. talking about someone who is generally good tempered but occasionally gets angry

    "He's usually good natured, but I've seen him angry _____."

Vocabulary

Academic Word List

Practice reading and saying aloud these vocabulary words. How many of the words do you already know?

1. **domestic** [də mĕs´ tĭk] adj. relating to the family or household

   All cultures have <u>domestic</u> routines and rituals.

2. **ethnic** [ĕth´ nĭk] adj. relating to a group of people that have the same racial, national, religious, linguistic, or cultural background

   Large nations often have many different <u>ethnic</u> groups.

3. **immigration** [ĭm´ ĭ grā´ shən] n. the act of moving to a foreign country to live

   There was great deal of <u>immigration</u> to the United States in the late 19th and early 20th centuries.

4. **implementation** [ĭm´ plə mən tā´ shən] n. the act of putting something into effect

   The <u>implementation</u> of social rules begins at an early age.

5. **impose** [ĭm pōz´] v. to place a burden or obligation on someone; to bring about by exercising authority; to force oneself on another

   Human society <u>imposes</u> rules of behavior on its members.
   The government <u>imposed</u> a new tax on the farmers.
   Problems sometimes occur in society when different groups try to <u>impose</u> their values on each other.

6. **integration** [ĭn tĭ grā´ shən] n. the act of bringing parts together into one whole

   The <u>integration</u> of various ethnic groups is a goal of large societies.

7. **interaction** [ĭn´ tər ăk´ shən] n. the process of communicating with, acting on, or affecting each other

   Culture sets the social rules for <u>interaction</u> between people.

8. **minorities** [mə nôr´ ĭ tēz] *or* [mə nŏr´ ĭ tēz] n. racial, political, religious, or other groups different from the majority of people in a country

   <u>Minorities</u> in societies are sometimes not given the same rights as others.

9. **reliance** [rĭ lī´ əns] n. the act of dependence

   A <u>reliance</u> on rules of behavior to keep order is found in all cultures.

10. **status** [stā´ təs] *or* [stăt´ əs] n. social, legal, or professional position relative to others; rank or standing

    Minorities sometimes have a lower <u>status</u> than others in society.

ACTIVITY ❹   *Vocabulary Practice*

Complete each sentence with a word from the Academic Word List on page 21.

1. Tacos are a dish from Mexico, so in the United States they are considered _____ food.

2. When there is no _____ between people, it is easy for them to misunderstand each other's behavior.

3. The _____ of the new courses into the school's anthropology program has given the students some interesting new choices.

4. _____ often complain that they are not treated equally by the majority in society.

5. The first _____ to the United States was from Europe. Later, people came from many other parts of the world.

6. All cultures have rules of behavior that they _____ on their members.

7. Immigrants often have a strong _____ on the traditions they bring from their native countries. These traditions make them feel more comfortable in their new homeland.

8. The _____ of laws in society is done by the government.

9. In some cultures, grandparents have very high _____ in the family, but in others they are not considered very important.

10. In some cultures women have all the _____ duties.

Word Forms

Like many words in English, some of the words in the Academic Word List have other forms in different parts of speech. For example, the noun *reliance* is *rely* as a verb, *reliable* and *reliant* as adjectives, and *reliably* as an adverb.

Here are some rules for making some different word forms. You will learn more rules about word forms in the chapters to come in this book.

1. The suffix **-tion**

   The suffix **-tion** can be added to many verbs to form nouns. Verbs with a final consonant + **e** drop the **e**, for example *activate / activation, reduce / reduction*. Sometimes a different vowel is added before **-tion**, for example, *compete / competition*. Conversely, when you see nouns that end in **-tion**, their verb form often ends in **e**, for example, *memorization / memorize*.

2. Changing adjectives to adverbs with **-ly**

   A common rule to change adjectives to adverbs is by adding the suffix **-ly** to the word, for example, *bad / badly, sure / surely, happy / happily* (if the word has a final **y**, the **y** is changed to **i**.)

3. The noun ending **-nce**

   Often when nouns with the **-nce** ending are made into adjectives, the **-ce** becomes a **t**, for example *defiance / defiant*.

Work with Word Forms

The words in the box are used in another form in the sentences below. Choose the appropriate word and add the word ending in parentheses to complete the sentences. Look back at the word form rules to help you. Then give the part of speech for the new word. The first one is done for you.

immigration	~~impose~~	interaction	ethnic
domestic	integration	reliance	status

1. The new work rules at the office were a big ___imposition___ (ition) on the employees, so they complained to the boss.

   Part of speech: __noun__

2. Money and education are common indicators of _____ (no change) in society.

   Part of speech: _____

3. People are social beings. They feel _____ (nt) on others in the community for their survival, and it is natural for them to _____ (ct) with each other.

   Parts of speech: _____ _____

4. People in large societies who are _____ (ally) different often find it difficult to feel accepted by the majority.

   Part of speech: _____

5. African Americans began to _____ (te) into schools for whites only in the American South in the 1950's. Until that time, blacks and whites went to separate schools.

   Part of speech: _____

6. The _____ (tion) of wild animals is dangerous. Some animals should not be pets in the home.

   Part of speech: _____

7. People _____ (te) to new countries looking for a better life.

   Part of speech: _____

Discourse Markers and Commonly Used Expressions

The English language includes a number of discourse markers and many commonly used phrases and expressions. Discourse markers are words that show us, for example, the places in a lecture where the speaker begins, changes topic or idea, or emphasizes differences or similarities. Speakers "mark" these places to make what they say easier to understand. Discourse markers are typically used to focus listeners' attention on the words that come after the discourse markers.

Common phrases and expressions are combinations of words that have particular meanings which clarify the material they refer to. Look at the charts below.

Discourse Marker	Function
my topic today is	Introduce
first and foremost	List
on top of that	Give further information
just what is meant by	Define
it goes without saying	Give background information

Common Phrases and Expressions		
the upshot of	with the aim of	part and parcel of

For a complete list of discourse markers and common expressions, see Appendix 2, page 127.

 **ACTIVITY 6**

Understand Discourse Markers and Commonly Used Expressions

The underlined words in the sentences below are discourse markers and phrases listed in the charts above. You will hear them in the upcoming mini-lecture. Write their meanings from the following list.

it is already understood	exactly the meaning of
~~the subject I want to talk about now~~	and even more
the consequence or result of	having the goal of
an important element	most importantly

1. <u>My topic today</u> is the bartering systems of nomadic peoples.

   <u>The subject I want to talk about now</u>

2. Can you explain <u>just what is meant by</u> the word "culture"?

   _____

3. There were no classes this week on Wednesday, Thursday, and Friday because of the snowstorm. It was great to have the time free, but <u>the upshot of</u> all this is that we will have to stay an extra half hour for all our classes next week.

_____

4. I'm taking an intensive Spanish course <u>with the aim of</u> moving in a year to work in Mexico.

_____

5. I have two final exams this week. <u>On top of that</u>, I have to work extra hours every day at my part-time job.

_____

6. Spending hours in the library every week is <u>part and parcel</u> of being a successful student.

_____

7. <u>It goes without saying</u> that if you don't do all the work in this class, you won't pass it.

_____

8. Language, <u>first and foremost</u>, is the way in which human beings are different from all other animals.

_____

Listen and Respond

ACTIVITY ❼

Listen to the Mini-Lecture

First Listening: Listen for Vocabulary You will hear a mini-lecture played two times. The first time, listen for vocabulary from the Academic Word List. Fill in the blanks in the first column with the words you hear. You will hear them in the order they are spoken. Then match them to their restatement in column 2.

1. … _____ among a group of human beings …

2. … different _____ populations …

3. … as a result of _____ …

4. … with the _____ of these new subcultures …

5. … some kind of _____ structure …

6. … rules _____ by the group …

7. … deciding _____ and leadership …

8. … the _____ of group decisions …

9. … out of a _____ on each other …

a. _____ family unit

b. _____ groups with a national identity different from that of the main national identity

c. _____ choosing social positions

d. _____ made necessary by the members

e. _____ doing what the people decide

f. _____ because of a dependence

g. _____ mixing together of new social groups

h. _____ communication between people

i. _____ consequence of new people entering a country

Second Listening: Listen and Outline Listen to the mini-lecture again. Take notes using the outline method you learned in Chapter 1.

Compare your notes with a partner's. Discuss any information that is different.

 ACTIVITY 8   *Answer Questions about the Mini-Lecture*

Use your notes from the lecture to answer these questions. You may want to read the questions, and then listen to the lecture again before answering.

1. What is often a cultural characteristic of large countries?

   _____

2. How do ethnic populations occur in large countries?

   _____

3. Which of the following is a characteristic shared by all cultures?
   a. only a mother and father raising children
   b. belief in God
   c. group status
   d. men and women sharing work responsibilities equally

4. What is a subculture?

   _____

5. Write the universal characteristic of culture that would apply to each of the following:

   ideas about stealing or lying   _____

   forming a government   _____

   music   _____

   the legal age for drinking alcohol _____

   fashions   _____

Stress and Pitch Patterns

When we speak we usually stress (emphasize) the content words — nouns, verbs, and adjective/adverbs — in our sentences, and de-emphasize the structure words — articles and prepositions. In this way, the listener can focus on the words that are important to the meaning of the statement. In the following sentences the bold words are stressed. Say the sentence aloud with emphasis on those words.

I had a **lot** of **homework** in **anthropology** class **last** night.

When we stress words, we also make certain parts of them different in pitch. Pitch is the highness or lowness of the sound in relation to the other sounds in the word or sentence. Did you notice, when you said the sentence above, if the pitch of the bold words went up or down? Look at the following stress and pitch marks of the sentence.

$$\qquad\uparrow\qquad\uparrow\qquad\qquad\qquad\uparrow$$

I had a **lot** of **homework** in anthropology class last night.
$$\qquad\qquad\qquad\downarrow$$

The pitch of the stressed word is higher when it has a single syllable, such as "lot". In all words with more than one syllable, the stressed syllable always has the highest pitch, such as in anthro<u>po</u>logy or <u>home</u>work.

ACTIVITY **9**

Listen for Stress and Pitch Patterns

Read the following sentences taken from the mini-lecture and underline the words you think should be stressed. Mark the parts of the words with ↑ if the pitch is higher than normal and ↓ if the pitch is lower than normal. Then listen to the recording and check your answers, correcting them if necessary. Notice that in most of these sentences the last content word is usually strongly stressed.

1. All human groups have domestic structures for raising children.

2. Cultural groups share a common language.

3. Humans have gender and age distinctions as a means of classification.

4. Marriage and family ties are a form of classifying members.

5. There are distinctions in the division of work that people do.

6. All people share a sense of the need for privacy.

7. Rules are imposed by the group on an individual's sexual behavior.

8. The group decides what is right and wrong for the members.

9. All groups wear some form of clothing or jewelry.

10. Games and humor are found in all cultures.

Vocabulary

Academic Word List

Practice reading and saying aloud these vocabulary words. How many do you already know?

1. **commitment** [kə mĭt´ mənt] n. a promise or an obligation to keep certain beliefs or follow a course of action

   People have a strong <u>commitment</u> to their cultural values.

2. **communication** [kə myoo´ nĭ kā´ shən] n. the exchange of thoughts, information, or messages

   Only human beings are capable of <u>communication</u> through written language.

3. **cycle** [sī´ kəl] n. a series of events that is periodically repeated

   Many Asian cultures believe that the birth/death <u>cycle</u> repeats itself with the soul continuing in a new body.

4. **emerge** [ĭ mûrj´] v. to rise out of something, such as water; to become known or visible

   The swimmer <u>emerged</u> from the water.
   Anthropologists see similar behaviors in all cultures that <u>emerge</u> from their rituals.

5. **grant** [grănt] v. to give or allow something as a favor or privilege. n. financial support or funding

   In many cultures, the right to marry must be <u>granted</u> by the father of the bride.
   The government gives occasional <u>grants</u> for scientists to do intensive educational research.

6. **initial** [ĭ nĭsh´ əl] adj. relating to or occurring at the beginning; first

   The <u>initial</u> results of the cross-cultural research showed strong differences in how the two cultures viewed the idea of success, but later it became clear that there were also some similarities.

7. **negative** [nĕg´ ə tĭv] adj. expressing denial or refusal; not positive

   Most cultures have <u>negative</u> associations with death.
   The anthropologist studied the positive and <u>negative</u> reactions of different ethnic groups to various concepts of masculinity and femininity.

8. **outcome** [out´ kŭm´] n. a final result

   The <u>outcome</u> of Coming of Age ceremonies for boys is that they are considered men by their social group.

9. **remove** [rĭ moov´] v. to move from a position or place; to take away

   In many marriage ceremonies, the bride wears a veil that she <u>removes</u> to kiss the groom after the wedding vows.

10. **task** [tăsk] n. a piece of work assigned or done as part of one's duties

    <u>Tasks</u> within the family unit are often assigned according to gender.

Vocabulary Practice with Word Forms

Use the word forms in the chart to complete the sentences below.

NOUN	VERB	ADJECTIVE	ADVERB
commitment	commit	committed	X
communication	communicate	communicative	communicatively
cycle	X	cyclical	cyclically
emergence	emerge	emergent	X
grant	grant	X	X
initiation	initiate	initial	initially
negativity, negation	negate	negative	negatively
outcome	X	X	X
removal	remove	removable	X
task	X	X	X

1. The four seasons of the year are _____.
2. Too much _____ in one's attitude can make it impossible to do anything.
3. The _____ of Western cultural traditions dates back to around 5,000 years ago in the Mediterranean area of the world.
4. It is difficult to know the _____ when different cultures come in contact with one another.
5. She was given a /an _____ of $15,000 by the government to study the languages and rituals of Native Americans of the Southwest.
6. In prehistoric societies, it was the man's _____ to hunt for food.
7. Native American men used to paint their faces before a battle and _____ the paint afterwards.
8. In wedding ceremonies in all cultures, a man and woman _____ themselves to each other for life.
9. _____, prehistoric people hunted and gathered food. Only later, when farming began, did civilizations begin to grow much larger.
10. For many thousands of years, people could only _____ orally. Written _____ is a recent development in human history.

ACTIVITY 11   *Make the Word Form Connections*

Study the patterns below. Then complete the word form chart with the patterns you see.

NOUN	VERB	ADJECTIVE	ADVERB
information	inform	informative	informatively
embarrassment	embarrass	embarrassed	embarrassedly
emergence	emerge	emergent	X
foolishness	fool	foolish	foolishly
removal	remove	removable	X
possibility	X	possible	possibly
communication	communicate	communicative	communicatively

1. _____ X invisible _____
2. _____ X _____ childishly
3. _____ harass _____ X
4. _____ _____ formulative _____
5. _____ retrieve _____ X
6. _____ diverge _____ X
7. reformation _____ _____ _____

ACTIVITY 12   *Define Discourse Markers and Commonly Used Expressions*

The underlined words in the sentences will be in the next lecture. Circle the answers that you think match their meanings. For a complete list of discourse markers and commonly used phrases and expressions, see Appendix 2, page 129.

1. All her studying <u>stems from</u> her desire to be an archeologist like her mother.
   a. comes from
   b. is unrelated to

2. The discovery of the art and jewels of Egyptian tombs <u>gave rise to</u> a new style of fashion called art deco.
   a. caused
   b. lifted

3. He was going to give his report on Iron Age tools, but another student was already doing it. <u>Instead of</u> that report, he did one on the cave drawings of Altamira.
   a. rather than
   b. in addition to

Key Concepts 2: Listening, Note Taking, and Speaking Across the Disciplines

4. She was given a grant to study totems in Alaska. <u>What's more</u>, she was guaranteed a position with the university when she finished her research.
   a. what else
   b. in addition

5. <u>Owing to</u> his many years alone studying runes in Scotland, he found it difficult to return to normal society.
   a. despite
   b. due to

6. <u>Today we are going to discuss</u> ancient tool-making techniques.
   a. next we will talk about
   b. let's begin class with

7. <u>After all is said and done</u>, it is obvious that human beings share many more similarities than differences.
   a. after all debate is finished
   b. in my opinion

8. I'm tired, but <u>that isn't to say</u> that I won't finish my homework before I go to bed.
   a. I can't say
   b. it doesn't mean

9. <u>Prior to</u> getting her Masters degree in Cultural Anthropology, she received her Baccalaureate degree in Sociology.
   a. before
   b. while

10. <u>Although</u> all cultures have words for colors, some cultures recognize more of them than others do.
    a. even though
    b. likely

Listen and Respond

ACTIVITY 13

Listen to the Extended Lecture

First Listening: Listen for Word Forms You will hear an extended lecture played two times. The first time, listen for word forms for each of the vocabulary words you have learned. Circle the words in the box that you hear. (You may want to review the word forms on page 29 before you listen.)

emergence	cyclical	commit	emerged
negative	removed	outcome	negativity
task	granted	initial	outcomes
communication	cycle	grants	removes
tasks	commitment	initiate	communicate

Second Listening: Listen and Take Notes Listen to the extended lecture again. Take notes using one of the methods you learned about in Chapter 1.

NOTE: If you use symbols instead of words to save time while taking notes, refer to Appendix 5 on pp. 139–140 for more information on using note-taking symbols.

Now compare your notes with a partner. Are your notes and your partner's similar? Did you miss some important information?

Answer Questions about the Extended Lecture

Use your notes from the lecture to answer these questions. You may want to read the questions, then listen to the lecture again before answering.

1. Which two supernatural categories would be considered the most similar? Why?

   _____

   _____

2. What is the difference in the way that Western cultures and Asian cultures generally view ghosts?

   _____

   _____

3. Which two categories believe that all things in the world have in them a supernatural force?

   _____

   _____

4. In which category of supernatural belief are there good and bad spirits in things?

   _____

5. Hinduism is polytheistic and Catholicism is monotheistic, yet the professor says they are similar. In what way?

   _____

   _____

Compare your answers with those of other students in the class.

Think Critically: Choose the Category

Use the extended lecture notes you took to match the following activities to the categories of supernatural beliefs stated in the lecture. Put the letter of the belief next to the activity. When you finish, compare your answers with a partner's.

a. Animatism	b. Animism	c. ancestral spirits
d. minor supernatural beings		e. gods and goddesses

1. _____ carrying something that brings you good luck

2. _____ trying to communicate with the dead

3. _____ feeling unlucky because a black cat crossed your path

4. _____ a belief in a spirit that controls the weather

5. _____ a belief that people have an aura, or spiritual energy, around their bodies

ACTIVITY **16**

Research and Summarize Topics

Rites of passage are ceremonies occurring in different cultures that show that a person has reached an important point of change in his or her life. They vary from culture to culture, but the following rites are quite common in most human societies:

- Coming of Age — reaching the age when a person is considered an adult
- Marriage
- Having children
- Retirement

Task

Choose a rite of passage in any culture you like in the world (it can be your own) and give a five-minute oral summary of it for the class. In your summary use as many discourse markers and common phrases and expressions as you can.

Guidelines

Do the following on your own, with a partner, or with a small group:

1. Look up the rite of passage in a dictionary or encyclopedia to get a broad sense of what it means.

2. Research your rite of passage further in the library or on the Internet.

3. Include these general elements in your presentation:
    - the fundamental meaning of the rite
    - where and when the rite is performed and by whom
    - the various steps involved and what each one means
    - a visual — poster, pictures, diagrams, drawings — to enhance your presentation. You might even want to use music if it is appropriate for your rite of passage.

4. Avoid reading from notes or a paper; instead, convey the meaning and steps of the ceremony in your own words as much as possible.

5. If you are working with a partner or a small group, make sure each person has an equal part in the presentation.

Research Beings from Folklore

Unless you are a Native American, your ancestors come from another part of the world. Use the library or Internet to find a supernatural being in the folklore from your part of the world. Prepare a two-page report about this being to put into a class booklet. Make note cards to give a five-minute presentation to the class. Be sure to include what the being meant in folklore, what powers it had, and a brief story that shows how those powers were used.

For more activities and information, go to the *Key Concepts* 2 website at *elt.heinle.com/keyconcepts*.

3 From Business: Business Ethics

BUS 1302
Business Ethics (3)

This course will introduce you to the ethical issues and rules of behavior in the business world today and will cover management/employee relations, fair hiring practices, and ethical guidelines in management, marketing, and negotiating.

Business is one of the most popular majors among community college and university students. One area of study in business programs that is receiving a lot of attention these days is business ethics, which deals with fair decision-making practices and appropriate behavior in the business world. Read the description on the left for a class in Business Ethics.

Now find a course description for an introductory business ethics course from your community college or university catalog. What similarities do the two courses have? What are the differences?

This chapter will help you understand some **key concepts** of business ethics, such as

- common issues of right and wrong between and within businesses

- methods for resolving ethical business problems

- ways for management and employees to work together to improve the workplace environment

- ethical issues in international business

You will also practice some academic skills for success.

Get Ready to Listen

Ethics deals with making decisions about what is the right thing to do in everyday situations. Ethics is based on moral values, which are beliefs about what is right and wrong in all situations, but often those moral values can come in conflict with ethical considerations. This may seem strange, but let's look at a common example of a "white lie," which is a small lie told to avoid hurting someone's feelings:

A young boy shows his mother a drawing he has done of their home. It is not very good, but the child spent quite a while on it and is eager for his mother's opinion. She can follow the moral rule that lying is always wrong, but as an adult, and a mother, she realizes her honesty about the drawing will hurt the child's feelings. What should she do? Her choice is one that weighs the absolute moral belief in always telling the truth against an ethical consideration of not hurting the child's feelings or discouraging him. Most parents in such a situation would tell the child they liked the drawing; in other words they would tell a "white lie" to make the child feel good.

ACTIVITY ❶ *Brainstorming and Discussion*

The situation with the child and the bad drawing is not difficult to decide. However, most ethical dilemmas are not so clear and simple. In the world of business, ethical decisions are constantly being made. Look at the following situations and write what you would do. Give your reasons. When you are finished, discuss your answers in small groups.

1. You are the owner of a large company and you need a new manager for a department. You have interviewed several people and narrowed your decision down to two of them. One is your brother's wife, whose qualifications for the job are generally equal to the other person's qualifications. Who do you hire?

    YOUR DECISION: _____

    REASONS: _____

    _____

2. You learn from your manager that your company doesn't hire women for high positions. This kind of discrimination is against the law and you don't like it. A newspaper reporter who also knows about the company's practice contacts you about it. If your company learns you said something to the reporter, you could lose your job. What do you do?

YOUR DECISION: _____

REASONS: _____

_____

3. New, stricter, clean-air standards that will cost more money will become the law in another two weeks. You are about to install some machines that do not meet those standards. If you install the machines without the expensive changes before the two-week deadline, they will be legal. Do you make the expensive changes to the machines or install them before the deadline?

YOUR DECISION: _____

REASONS: _____

_____

4. You have a very successful business, and you pay your employees the minimum wage allowed by law. Because of recent increases in the cost of living, it is obvious that this amount of money would be difficult to live on for your employees with families. They come to you to ask for more money. What do you do?

YOUR DECISION: _____

REASONS: _____

_____

5. You do business with companies overseas. In some of these countries, gifts of money are considered a normal part of doing business, but the laws of your country consider such gifts to be bribes, which are illegal. You know that if you do not offer these gifts, the companies will choose not to do business with you. The gifts would be easy for you to give secretly. What do you do?

YOUR DECISION: _____

REASONS: _____

_____

6. One of your colleagues at work has made some comments about how attractive your body is. You don't like it, and under the government guidelines for sexual harassment, you can report this person to your company. What do you do? (Do the answers in your group differ between men and women?)

YOUR DECISION: _____

REASONS: _____

_____

Listen and Respond

Listen to Conversations

You will hear some short conversations. Listen for the expressions and phrasal verbs listed in the box. Write the ones you hear in each conversation. Then circle the answer that gives the correct meaning.

get away with	look over	take for granted	take up
take advantage of	gets down to	make do	

1. _____
   a. do less work
   b. use something that gives you an extra benefit
   c. not go to the beach
   d. use in another way

2. _____
   a. avoid a negative result when not doing what is required or expected
   b. go somewhere
   c. take something with you
   d. get a grant for the course

3. _____
   a. gets to the end
   b. takes something with you
   c. lowers
   d. gives serious attention to

4. _____
   a. look beyond
   b. finish
   c. review
   d. find something to look at

5. _____
   a. make more than she can do
   b. use what she has even if it's not enough
   c. make what she does
   d. try to find more

6. _____
   a. change your idea
   b. take the course
   c. believe something you don't know for certain
   d. take the course but not grant all the material to the professor

7. _____
   a. continue
   b. get good at
   c. start a new, regular activity
   d. lift

Vocabulary

Academic Word List

Practice reading and saying aloud these vocabulary words. How many of the words do you already know?

1. **circumstance** [sûr´ kəm stăns´] n. a condition, situation, or event usually connected with and usually affecting another event

    Under the present <u>circumstances</u>, it is not likely that the school will have enough money for the new library.

2. **contribution** [kŏn´ trĭ byōō´ shən] n. the act of giving or supplying

    That company gives <u>contributions</u> to charity organizations.

3. **coordination** [kō ôr´ dn ā´ shən] n. the act of working together efficiently, in a common cause or effort, in a planned, harmonious way

    For a business to be successful, it needs <u>coordination</u> between its various departments.

4. **corporate** [kôr´ pər ĭt] or [kôr´prĭt] adj. relating to a large business organization

    Product safety is a <u>corporate</u> responsibility.

5. **job** [jŏb] n. a position at which a person works for pay; a task that must be done

    The <u>job</u> requires a lot of knowledge about sales.
    It is my son's <u>job</u> to wash the family car on Saturdays.

6. **occupational** [ŏk´ yə pā´ shən əl] adj. relating to a job

    Wearing a hardhat is an <u>occupational</u> requirement on construction sites.

7. **parameter** [pə răm´ ĭ tər] n. a fixed limit or boundary

    The government created stricter <u>parameters</u> for doing business with overseas countries.

8. **partnership** [pärt´ nər shĭp´] n. a relationship based on two or more people or entities working for a common enterprise, particularly in business

    The two companies formed a <u>partnership</u> to increase their profits.

9. **specify** [spĕc´ ə fī´] v. to state clearly or in detail

    The new rules <u>specify</u> that smoking will not be allowed in the building.

10. **sum** [sŭm] n. a number obtained as a result of adding numbers; the whole amount, quantity, or number

    The <u>sum</u> of two and two is four.
    He has to pay the owner the entire <u>sum</u> at one time if he wants to buy that car.

ACTIVITY 3

Vocabulary Practice with Word Forms

The words in the box are the Academic Word List vocabulary in different parts of speech. Choose the correct word to complete each sentence. Make changes for singular/plural or third person when necessary. Use each word only once.

Nouns:	corporation	occupation	specification
Verbs:	contribute	coordinate	
Adjectives:	circumstantial	coordinated	specific
Adverbs:	circumstantially		specifically

1. Ethics can sometimes be _____. It often depends on the particular situation.

2. She doesn't have much money, but she _____ to the cancer foundation every year.

3. If you want me to buy a shirt for him for his birthday present, please be very _____ about what he likes.

4. That company needs to _____ its communications between the design and marketing departments to succeed.

5. We need the _____ for the new product before we start making it.

6. A big _____ has an advantage over a small business.

7. The manager stated _____ that no shorts were allowed to be worn at work.

8. There is no direct proof that the company was involved in price-fixing, but a lot of things point _____ in that direction.

9. Nursing is an example of a medical _____.

10. If we all work together in a _____ effort, I think we can succeed.

Discourse Markers and Commonly Used Expressions

Study these discourse markers and phrases that you will hear in the mini-lecture.

Discourse Markers	Function
to begin	Listing
all in all	Summarizing
as far as I'm concerned	Giving opinion
it's worth mentioning	Emphasizing
all that aside	Shifting topics

Commonly Used Expressions	
It's all very well and good	Slowly but surely
Get the ball rolling	Miss the point

In the left column are discourse markers and commonly used expressions from the lists above. Read the sentences below with these words underlined. Then match the discourse markers and expressions with their meanings in the right column.

1. _____ to begin
2. _____ it's all very well and good … but
3. _____ as far as I'm concerned
4. _____ slowly but surely
5. _____ get the ball rolling
6. _____ all in all
7. _____ miss the point
8. _____ it is worth mentioning that
9. _____ all that aside

a. it is important
b. start something
c. first
d. in my opinion
e. disregarding that
f. it's okay, however
g. done completely over time
h. generally
i. not understand

1. To begin, let's look at the test schedule for this course.

2. It's all very well and good to want to lose weight, but you should be careful how you do it.

3. As far as I'm concerned, his behavior is inexcusable.

4. Slowly but surely, my grandfather recovered from his operation.

5. Everyone is here for the meeting, so let's get the ball rolling.

6. All in all, ethics training has helped this company.

7. I think you missed the point, so I will explain it again.

8. It is worth mentioning that companies with fair-hiring practices are as successful as companies that don't have them.

9. The plane trip was terrible and we couldn't rent a car, but all that aside, it was a great vacation.

Listen and Respond

Listen to the Mini-Lecture

 First Listening: Listen for Vocabulary You will hear a mini-lecture played two times. The first time, listen for vocabulary from the Academic Word List and discourse markers and commonly used expressions from Activity 4. Circle the words or phrases that you hear in the lecture.

specific – specify	partner – partnership
circumference – circumstances	occasional – occupational
parameters – partners	all in all – all told
controversial – contributions	job – chop
corporate – corporal	misses the mark – misses the point

Second Listening: Listen and Take Notes Listen to the mini-lecture again. Take notes using one of the note-taking methods you learned about in Chapter 1.

Compare your notes with those of a partner. Discuss any information that is different.

Answer Questions about the Mini-Lecture

Use your notes from the lecture to answer these questions. You may want to read the questions, then listen to the lecture again before answering.

1. The teacher wants to specify what is ethically right and wrong in the business world. (circle one)   TRUE   FALSE

2. Why is ethical behavior in the business world so difficult to define?

   _____

   _____

3. What does the teacher want to do with this class?

   _____

   _____

4. What areas of ethical behavior have some companies already tried to find solutions for? Have they been successful?

   _____

   _____

5. Why do employees resist training courses in ethics?

   _____

   _____

6. What is one reason why today's business organizations need ethics training?

   _____

   _____

7. What is necessary for a business organization's success?

   _____

   _____

LISTENING 3   ● **Pronunciation**

Stress For Meaning

Many verbs in English can be joined with prepositions to make words that are either compound nouns (*handout*) or verb phrases (*hand out*). In addition, some words in English can be nouns (*con*tract) or verbs (*con*tract or con*tract*) depending on how their syllables are stressed. The meanings of these words are often, but not always, similar.

Study the two sets of sentences with the stressed parts in italics.

The teacher began to **hand *out*** (verb) the tests.

The teacher gave us a business survey ***hand*out** (noun).

The homeless man asked me for a ***hand*out** (noun).

"Hand out" in the first sentence is two words and means "to distribute." "Handout" in the second sentence means "printed material that is distributed." However, "handout" in the third sentence has the particular meaning of "charity."

Study these sentences.

The ***contract*** (noun) was signed last week.

We need to ***contract*** (verb) a new shipping company for our products.

Turtles ***contract*** (verb) their heads into their shells when they sense danger.

Jaime ***contracted*** (verb) malaria while traveling last summer.

"Contract" in the first sentence means "a legal document signed in business agreements." In the second sentence "contract" means "to make a legal business agreement." However, in the third sentence, "contract" means "to pull away from." "Contract" in the fourth sentence means "to become infected with."

Rules for Stress

1. In nouns that are joined with prepositions to make one word, the first word is stressed (***hand*out** = printed material).

2. When the words are separate and make a verb phrase, the word that follows the verb is stressed (**hand *out*** = to distribute).

3. In words with two syllables that can be used as a noun or verb, the nouns often stress the first syllable (***contract*** = agreement) and verbs often stress the second syllable (**contract** = to make a legal agreement OR to pull away from physically).

Listen for Stress

A. Using the rules on the previous page, listen to the sentences and number the words a or b in the order that you hear them. Then circle S if the meaning of the words is similar or D if their meaning is different.

NOUNS	VERBS		
1. __*b*__ workout	__*a*__ work out	S	Ⓓ
2. _____ holdup	_____ hold up	S	D
3. _____ holdout	_____ hold out	S	D
4. _____ hookup	_____ hook up	S	D
5. _____ runaround	_____ run around	S	D
6. _____ shutdown	_____ shut down	S	D
7. _____ *im*port	_____ im*port*	S	D

B. Now listen to the sentences again. Write the words you hear next to the meanings that go with them.

1. __workout__   a lot of physical exercise

   __work out__   resolve a problem

2. _____   lift

   _____   delay

3. _____   refusing to accept

   _____   offer, give

4. _____   connection

   _____   meet

5. _____   go to many different places

   _____   long, intentionally confusing process

6. _____   the ending of all activity

   _____   to close

7. _____   bring into the country a product from another country

   _____   a product from another country sold in your country

Vocabulary

Academic Word List

Practice reading and saying aloud these vocabulary words. How many do you already know?

1. **annual** [an´ yo͞o əl] adj. happening or done every year

   The <u>annual</u> deadline to pay income tax in the U.S. is April fifteenth.

2. **compensation** [kŏm´ pən sā´ shən] n. something given or received as a payment or to balance a loss

   Businesses give <u>compensation</u> to employees who are hurt on the job.

3. **deduction** [dĭ dŭk´ shən] n. an amount that is taken away from another amount; a conclusion that is reached from a general principle

   The U.S. Government takes a Social Security <u>deduction</u> from people's paychecks.
   The engineers made a <u>deduction</u> from the laws of physics that the new plane would fly.

4. **document** [dŏk´ yə mənt] n. a written or printed paper that can be used to give evidence

   A rental contract is a legal <u>document</u>.

5. **fund** [fŭnd] n. a sum of money used for a certain purpose

   The government gave emergency <u>funds</u> to the flood victims.

6. **output** [out´ po͝ot´] n. an amount of something produced, especially during a given amount of time

   The new rules in the factory increased the workers' <u>output</u> by 10 percent.

7. **phase** [fāz] n. a distinct stage of development

   The first <u>phase</u> of the new sales plan will be direct mail advertisements.

8. **professional** [prə fĕsh´ ə nəl] adj. relating to jobs that require a specialized skill

   The practice of law is a <u>professional</u> career.

9. **register** [rĕg´ ĭ stər] v. to enroll, record, or take note of

   She <u>registered</u> for evening classes at the university.

10. **shift** [shĭft] v. to transfer from one place or position to another. n. a period in which a group of workers are on duty at the same time

    The company <u>shifted</u> the production jobs to factories overseas. (v)
    He gets home late because he works the evening <u>shift</u>. (n)

ACTIVITY 8

Vocabulary Practice

Match the parts of the sentences. The words in bold are from the Academic Word List you just studied. The first one has been done for you.

1. A marriage certificate is	employees receive	holiday in the United States.
2. The fourth of July is	**shifted**	advice to a business.
3. The law requires that	**output**	**document**.
4. Scientists use	**register**	fair **compensation** for their work.
5. The moon's lit shape	an **annual**	various **phases** each month.
6. The company's	a **fund**	its operations to China.
7. That business has	physical laws to make	it uses for emergencies.
8. A tax consultant offers	a legal	deductions.
9. A student has to	**professional**	for classes.
10. That company	goes through	has increased by 15% this year.

ACTIVITY 9

Work with Discourse Markers and Commonly Used Expressions

The following underlined words are in the extended lecture. Complete the sentences with the definitions in the box. Then circle two of the three items below each sentence that could most likely be used with the underlined words.

in a difficult or bad situation	ignoring	finish
a complete commitment to something	understand	if
~~an important time of change in life~~	pay all	
in my opinion	using common sense	

1. Graduation from college is a <u>turning point</u> for a person.
   an important time of change in life

   a *turning point:* (marriage) Christmas vacation (retirement)

2. She decided to join the army <u>without regard to</u> her parents wishes for her to stay in school. _____

   without regard to: danger someone's feelings somewhere

3. <u>Supposing that</u> you were given a million dollars, how would you spend it?

   _____

   Supposing that: it doesn't rain I pass the test the sun rises

4. "I spent too much money this month and can't pay the rent. I'm in a fix."

   _____

   in a fix: stuck in traffic and can't get to the meeting

   unsure what you want for dinner   forgot your wedding anniversary

5. Practically speaking, it's better to study a little each night than to try and
   learn it all the night before the test._____
   Practically speaking: this vacation will cost less than the other one
   people should follow their dream   saving money is a smart idea

6. He left the restaurant suddenly and I had to foot the bill. _____
   foot the bill: going in the hospital and not having any insurance
   parents' supporting their kids' through college   roommates' sharing rent

7. If you ask me, it's better to get paid a little less for a job you like than to get
   paid a little more for a job you don't. _____
   if you ask me: this shirt looks better on you than that one
   this course is very interesting   some cars are more expensive than others

8. I'm going to break up with him if he doesn't marry me. I told him it's all or
   nothing! _____
   all or nothing: putting a little money on the stock market
   using your entire savings to make your company succeed
   betting the rest of your money on one hand of poker

9. Okay, it's been a long day. It's time to wrap up and go home.

   _____

   wrap up: a police investigation   a gift   a meeting

10. I can't get a grasp of the teacher's instructions. What does she want us to
    do? _____
    get a grasp of: a problem   a time limit   a meaning

Listen and Respond

ACTIVITY 10

Listen to the Extended Lecture

First Listening: Listen for Vocabulary You will hear an extended lecture played two times. The first time, listen for vocabulary from the Academic Word List and fill in the blanks. You will hear the words in the order they are listed below.

1. … firing, _____, working conditions

2. … privacy and respect. _____ managerial …

3. … productive _____ …

4. … company secrets or _____

5. … employees to _____ for training …

6. … a final _____ of this training

7. … overstated their _____ earnings …

8. … standard business _____

9. … U.S. laws forbid _____ _____ for such purposes …

Second Listening: Listen and Take Notes Listen to the extended lecture again. Take notes using one of the methods you learned about in Chapter 1.

Compare your notes with those of a partner. Discuss any information that is different.

Answer Questions about the Extended Lecture

Use your notes from the lecture to answer these questions. You may want to read the questions, then listen to the lecture again before answering.

1. Put these words together to list the four issues of ethical treatment of employees that should concern managers.

compensation	firing	conditions	privacy
working	respect	hiring	

   - _____ and _____

   - _____ _____

   - _____ and _____

   - _____

2. Now put the words from the blanks next to the example that applies to them below. There may be more than one possible answer.

   a. A manager reads the e-mail of one of the employees when she leaves her desk for a minute. _____

   b. A boss tells an employee that she is getting fat. _____

   c. An airline advertises for women under 25 years old to be flight attendants. _____

   d. An employee loses her job because she has a baby. _____

   e. A company tells employees that they must do more work for the same pay. _____

   f. The company's electric bill is high, so it turns down the air conditioning. _____

3. What are the two areas the teacher mentions about how employees might unethically treat the organization?

   _____ _____

4. What have some companies done in response to the issues of employee treatment ?

   _____

5. What example does the teacher give about unethical company treatment of customers?
   a. selling products that don't work
   b. charging too much for products the customers must have
   c. giving bribes to customers
   d. not having enough products for all the customers

6. How can doing business internationally create an ethical problem for businesses?

   _____

   _____

Think Critically: Review a Contract

You are deciding whether to accept a job being offered to you. Review your lecture notes on ethical issues to help you examine the following parts of the contract you would have to sign. Decide which area of ethical business practices each section relates to and put any objections in the spaces provided after each section. Give your reasons for these objections, and change the contract to make it more acceptable to you. If you think a section is acceptable, then write "no changes." When you finish, get into groups and compare your decisions.

JONES
&
JONES

234 BANBURN STREET
CROSSRIDGE, CT 56789

CONTRACT

All of the following are requirements for Party B (employee). If any of the requirements are violated, then Party A (employer) has the **option** to **terminate** this contract.

1. Party B will work an 8-hour day with half an hour for lunch.

   _____

   _____

2. Party B will work additional hours when necessary. This additional time will be paid for with an increased **wage**.

   _____

   _____

3. Party B will not use the office phones for personal calls or computers for personal **correspondence**.

   _____

   _____

4. Party A does not want any smokers in the company. If it is learned that Party B is a smoker, Party B's contract will be terminated immediately.

   _____

   _____

5. Any accusations of sexual harassment against Party B by another employee will result in immediate termination of Party B's contract.

   _____

   _____

6. If Party B wants to terminate his/her contract before the time **stipulated**, he/she must **give notice** at least one-and-a-half months before the desired termination date. Any notice received that is not within this **deadline** will result in Party B's receiving 75% of his/her normal wage for the time he/she remains with the company.

   _____

   _____

7. If Party B violates any of these requirements, Party A has the right to terminate Party B's contract and give two weeks' notice to Party B.

   _____

   _____

option — the power or right of choice

terminate — to bring to an end or halt

wage — salary, payment made to a worker for work done

correspondence — communication through the exchange of letters

stipulated — to specify or demand as a condition of an agreement or contract

give notice — inform a landlord or employer of one's intention to leave; inform an employee of termination of his/her contract

deadline — a time limit, a date set by which something must be done

---

SPEAKING   ● Extemporaneous Speaking

ACTIVITY **13**

Give an Extemporaneous Speech

Extemporaneous speaking means to speak without time to prepare your thoughts. Another way to say this is "to speak off the top of your head."

Task

Deliver a two-minute extemporaneous speech to the class about a topic your teacher gives you. In your speech use as many discourse markers and common phrases and expressions as you can.

1. Your teacher will assign each student a number.

2. Then your teacher will read a statement* and say a number.

3. If your number is called, stand up and give a two-minute extemporaneous response to the statement. The idea is to keep talking and not worry about whether you are speaking perfect English.

4. Your teacher will call another number, and that student will give a two-minute response to what the first student said, either agreeing or disagreeing.

5. After both students have spoken about the topic, any student may offer a comment.

6. The teacher makes another statement and the class begins the sequence again.

* For possible statements, go to *elt.heinle.com/keyconcepts.*

> **Example:** Your teacher might say, "People who do hard physical labor should get more money than people who work in an office all day."
>
> You can respond by agreeing or disagreeing. For example, you might say:
>
> *"I disagree. <u>In my opinion</u>, anyone can do physical work, but if you work in an office you have to have some particular skills. You have to have education and know how to use a computer. And this kind of work can be very stressful, for example …"*
>
> After two minutes the teacher will call another number. That student will have two minutes to respond. For example, the second student could say:
>
> *"I disagree with _____ (first student's name) because hard physical work is just as necessary as office work. You can't have an office unless someone builds it for you …"*
>
> Or the second student could agree with the first and give more reasons.

NOTE: People have different opinions about the appropriateness of verbally disagreeing with others. Some of us think that it's more polite to avoid such disagreement. However, an important thing to remember when you are doing this kind of exercise is that what you say is only a difference of opinion and not personal; this is illustrated by the use of "*in my opinion*". In order to truly discuss the issues, you should say what you are thinking while being respectful of others' opinions.

Strategies for Speaking Extemporaneously

Now let's look at some strategies for extemporaneous speaking.

1. As you consider the statement you hear, ask yourself if you agree or disagree and why.

2. Begin speaking by repeating the statement.

3. Then use an introductory phrase, such as:

In my opinion	It's a tough question	It seems to me
I believe	I don't have experience about this, but	
I know from my experience that		

4. Use examples or personal stories, if you can, to show your point.

5. Because there is a two-minute time limit, you need to get your ideas out quickly. Try to keep talking and let one thought lead to the next.

6. End with a summary or conclusion statement of your ideas or opinions.

7. Review the discourse markers, common phrases and expressions, and Academic Word List vocabulary from this chapter and try to use some of them in your remarks.

In your speech, use as many discourse markers and common phrases and expressions as you can.

 For more activities and information, go to the *Key Concepts* 2 website at *elt.heinle.com/keyconcepts*.

ENG 1102
Freshman English II (3)

Applying the skills practiced in ENG 1101, Freshman English II focuses on the persuasive and literary-based critical and evaluative skills of English composition. ENG 1102 contains readings in poetry, short stories, plays, and other literary works. Analysis of these genres in the forms of essays and a documented research paper is required. (Prerequisite: ENG 1101)

4 From Language Arts: English Literature

Regardless of their major, most colleges require students to take two semesters of English courses. An introduction to literature course covers various types of literature, but more importantly, it requires students to use critical thinking skills that they will need in order to succeed in academics and in their professional lives.

Read the course description above, then find a description for an English literature course from your community college or university catalog. What similarities do the two courses have? What are the differences?

This chapter will help you understand some **key concepts** of literature, such as

- plot analysis
- point of view and narrator
- story setting

You will also practice some academic skills for success.

Get Ready to Listen

ACTIVITY ❶   *Brainstorming and Discussion*

Answer the questions below. When you have finished, share your answers with the rest of the class.

1. What is one of your favorite books?

   _____

2. In one sentence, write down the main idea of the book.

   _____

3. Where does the story take place?

   _____

4. When does the story take place?

   _____

5. Who is the main character of the story?

   _____

6. Why did you enjoy the book so much?

   _____

Listen and Respond

Divisible (Separable) Phrasal Verbs

As you have learned, a phrasal verb is a combination of a verb and preposition (particle) whose meaning is usually different from the meaning of the verb alone. There are two main categories of phrasal verbs: those that can be divided and those that cannot. Divisible phrasal verbs are usually separated by a noun or a pronoun. Sample divisible phrasal verbs include:

I want to look over my notes before the test. pronoun **I want to look (them) over before the test.**	look over (to review or study)
Could you turn off the TV? pronoun **Could you turn (it) off?**	turn off (to switch a control so a device is not on)

NOTE: For a complete list of phrasal verbs, see Appendix 3, page 132.

ACTIVITY ❷   *Listen to Conversations*

Listen to the short conversations. Try to understand the meaning of the phrasal verbs based on the context. Then circle the best answer.

1. The phrase <u>bring up</u> has something to do with
   a. writing something
   b. asking something
   c. summarizing something

2. The phrase <u>hold up</u> is connected to
   a. energy   b. time
   c. understanding

3. You can <u>look</u> something <u>up</u> by
   a. checking in the classroom   b. visiting the professor
   c. searching in a textbook

4. In this dialogue, the phrase <u>make out</u> refers to
   a. understanding something   b. writing something
   c. researching something

5. Someone who <u>points</u> something <u>out</u> is usually
   a. hiding something   b. understanding something
   c. explaining something

6. When you <u>use</u> something <u>up</u>, you probably
   a. have to stop what you're doing   b. enjoy what you're doing
   c. need to continue what you're doing

7. If something is <u>shutting down</u>, it is usually
   a. very busy   b. broken
   c. closing

ACTIVITY 3   *Review Phrasal Verbs*

Circle the correct phrasal verb in the dialogue below. Then practice reading the dialogue aloud with a partner.

1. *Joann:* Hey Bob. I hate to (bring this up / use this up), but I can't study with you tonight. I've got to work.

2. *Bob:* I'm sorry, what? It's so loud in here that I couldn't (point out / make out) what you said. Did you say that you can't study with me?

3. *Joann:* Yeah. I've (shut down / used up) all my days off this week, so I have to go to work.

4. *Bob:* That's okay Joann. This won't (point me out / hold me up). I'll study alone.

5. *Joann:* Thanks for understanding, Bob. If you want, I can (look up / bring up) the literary terms in the morning before class and share my notes with you.

6. *Bob:* That would be great, thanks. Wait. Dr. Yost (held up / pointed out) that the glossary in the back of the book has some of the best definitions. You should probably use that.

7. *Joann:* That's good to know. OK. I've got to get something to eat before the kitchen (uses up / shuts down). See you tomorrow before class.

Vocabulary

Academic Word List

Practice reading and saying aloud these vocabulary words. How many of the words do you already know?

1. **academic** [ăkˊ ə dĕmˊ ĭk] adj. relating to a school or college

   The <u>academic</u> requirements of my English class are a lot more difficult than my other classes this semester.

2. **comment** [kŏmˊ ĕnt] n. a written note or remark that explains, interprets, or gives an opinion on something. v. to make a comment or remark

   My teacher's <u>comments</u> on my first essay draft were helpful. (n)
   I don't like it when my teacher <u>comments</u> in red all over my paper. (v)

3. **convention** [kən vĕnˊ shən] n. a formal meeting of a group for a particular purpose; general agreement on or acceptance of certain practices or attitudes

   The <u>convention</u> for English teachers is in late March this year.
   There are two main <u>conventions</u> when writing a bibliography in college: the *APA Style Manual* and the *MLA Style Manual*.

4. **dimension** [dĭ mĕnˊ shən] or [dī mĕnˊ shən] n. the measurement of a length, width, or thickness; the extent or magnitude

   Shakespeare's works are considered literature of grand <u>dimensions</u>.

5. **framework** [frāmˊ wûrk] n. a structure that shapes or supports something; a fundamental structure, as for a written work or a system of ideas

   The study of literature is a good <u>framework</u> on which to practice critical thinking.

6. **illustrate** [ĭlˊ ə strātˊ] or [ĭ lŭsˊ trātˊ] v. to make something clear or explain, as by using examples; to provide something with pictures or diagrams that explain or decorate

   By getting an A on his report, Joe has clearly <u>illustrated</u> that he understands the main concepts of Edgar Allen Poe's short stories.
   Instead of taking notes, James <u>illustrated</u> his notebook with diagrams of the lecture material.

7. **principal** [prĭnˊ sə pəl] adj. first in rank, degree, or importance

   The <u>principal</u> character in "The Necklace" is Madame Loisel.

8. **sex** [sĕks] n. gender

   For many years, women writers adopted pen names of the opposite <u>sex</u> in order to sell their books.

9. **sufficient** [sə fĭshˊ ənt] adj. as much as is needed; enough

   We didn't have <u>sufficient</u> time to finish our in-class essays.

10. **technique** [tĕk nēkˊ] n. a method for performing a complicated task, as in a science or an art

    There are many <u>techniques</u> to portray the tone of a story.

ACTIVITY 4 **Vocabulary Practice**

Circle the Academic Word List word that best completes each sentence. Some of the word forms have been changed. Use your dictionary if necessary.

1. One of the best _____ of a tragedy is Shakespeare's "Hamlet."
   a. techniques   b. illustrations

2. The instructor angrily _____ on the fact that we didn't turn in our essays on time.
   a. illustrated   b. commented

3. Do you understand the new _____ rules for the College of English?
   a. sufficient   b. academic

4. The formal _____ of writing are very different from what I'm used to when I communicate through e-mail.
   a. conventions   b. frameworks

5. The _____ theme of the short story was that men who are greedy suffer in the long term.
   a. dimensional   b. principal

6. This poem was one-_____; it was flat and did not contain a single element of tone or theme.
   a. dimensional   b. sex

7. For thousands of years, actors of the female _____ were not allowed to perform on stage.
   a. framework   b. sex

8. We didn't have _____ time to fully analyze Robert Frost's poem in class today.
   a. sufficient   b. academic

9. The American writer Poe often used the _____ of setting to create a tone of tragedy in his short stories.
   a. comment   b. technique

10. Within the _____ of classic literature, many of today's top authors wouldn't be considered successful.
    a. framework   b. illustration

Vocabulary Practice with Word Forms

The words in the chart are different forms — depending on their part of speech — of the Academic Word List vocabulary. Complete the chart with the correct word forms.

NOUN	VERB	ADJECTIVE	ADVERB
academic, academia	X	academic	_____
comment, commentary	comment	X	X
convention	convene	conventional	_____
dimensions	X	_____	dimensionally
framework	X	X	X
_____	illustrate	illustrated	X
principal	X	principal	_____
_____	publish	published	X
sex	X	_____	sexily
sufficiency	suffice	sufficient	_____

Discourse Markers

The following is a list of discourse markers you will hear in the mini-lecture.

Discourse Markers	Function
Today we're going to look at	Introducing
next	Listing
in other words	Clarifying
Let me end by saying …	Concluding

NOTE: For a complete list of discourse markers and commonly used expressions, see Appendix 2, page 129.

Listen and Respond

Listen to the Mini-Lecture

First Listening: Listen for Vocabulary and Discourse Markers You will hear a mini-lecture played two times. The first time, listen for the discourse markers from the box on the previous page. Put a check mark next to the phrases below that you hear. Only four of them appear in this lecture.

_____ Today we are going to consider   _____ Today we're going to look at

_____ Near   _____ Now

_____ In other words   _____ For instance,

_____ To sum up,   _____ Let me end by saying

Second Listening: Listen and Take Notes Listen to the mini-lecture again. Take notes using one of the note-taking methods you practiced in Chapter 1.

Compare your notes with those of a partner. Discuss any information that is different.

Answer Questions about the Mini-Lecture

Use your notes from the lecture to answer these questions. You may want to read the questions, then listen to the lecture again before answering.

1. How does the teacher begin the lecture?
   a. Giving an example of good literature
   b. Talking about movies
   c. Defining the elements of literature
   d. Asking questions about literature

2. Write at least two of the formal elements the teacher discusses.

   _____

3. Why is it important to understand the formal elements of literature?
   a. to appreciate the story
   b. to analyze the theme
   c. to explain how the elements work together

4. What are two examples of characters given in the lecture? _____

   _____

5. According to the teacher, setting can be a _____ or a

   _____ .

6. In your own words, write a definition of the word plot. _____

   _____

   _____

7. What three elements of literature are fundamental to understanding a story's universal idea?
   a. plot, theme, and setting
   b. setting, point of view, and character
   c. plot, setting, and character
   d. narrator, theme, and setting

LISTENING 3 ● Pronunciation

Pauses

When lecturers speak, they often introduce new material to the audience. Sometimes the new information is given in a straightforward way, with the lecturer clearly pointing out the definition of a new idea. Other times, however, the speaker pauses immediately after introducing a new idea. The phrase that follows this pause is usually a short definition or an example of the new thought. This is called a parenthetical explanation. Read this example.

> **Setting, (pause) the location, time, and props that are described in a story, (pause) can help you understand the theme of a story as much as the plot.**

In the following activity, you will listen for pauses in statements from the lectures. These pauses will signal a definition or example of the information being presented.

Listen for Pauses

As you listen to the following statements from the mini-lecture and the extended lecture, draw a vertical line where you hear a pause. Then underline the explanation or example that follows. Practice reading the phrases aloud, pausing where you have drawn the vertical lines. The first one has been done for you.

1. First, defining the elements of literature helps us characterize its form, | <u>what specific conventions a story uses.</u>

2. These characters may be people of either sex, animals, or even landscapes of nature, a young doctor, a lost fish, etc.

3. Setting may be any number of places or times, real places, eras of the past, imagined environments, or the imagination itself.

4. These fundamental ingredients, characters, settings, and plot provide readers with a basic sense of the story's theme, the universal idea that the story is trying to show.

5. As apparent as these elements may be, understanding that they always work together with the story's other elements, narrator, point of view, themes, images, symbols, language, style, and tone, is critically important.

6. This is an error because the narrator is a part of the story too, part of what is *told*, of what is conveyed or produced by the story.

Vocabulary

Academic Word List

Practice reading and saying aloud these vocabulary words. How many do you already know?

1. **alternative** [ôl tûr´ nə tĭv] n. one or two or more possibilities to choose from. adj. allowing a choice between two or more possibilities

   At our college, taking a Victorian literature course is an <u>alternative</u> to taking a course in modern British literature. (n)
   Students of literature should always look for <u>alternative</u> analyses of literature. (adj)

2. **apparent** [əp păr´ ənt] *or* [ə pâr´ ənt] adj. obvious; appearing to be something, but not necessarily so

   It is <u>apparent</u> that Shakespeare enjoyed writing tragic plays.

3. **attitude** [ăt´ ĭ tōōd´] n. a point of view or state of mind with regard to someone or something

   The reading public's <u>attitude</u> towards certain forms of literature changes with the times.

4. **contrast** [kən trăst´] *or* [kŏn´ trăst´] v. to compare differences between two things. n. a difference between things that are compared

   My research paper <u>contrasted</u> the tragic heroes Hamlet and Oedipus. (v)
   The <u>contrast</u> between Hamlet and Oedipus was the topic of today's lecture. (n)

5. **criteria** (pl) [krī tîr´ ē ə] n. rules or standards on which a judgment can be based

   An instructor's <u>criteria</u> for essay writing can include content, organization, thesis, and grammar.

6. **error** [ĕr´ ər] n. a mistake; something that is incorrect, wrong, or false

   My essay only contained two grammatical <u>errors</u>.

7. **goal** [gōl] n. objective; the purpose one works for

   One of the <u>goals</u> of a literature class should be a better understanding of the elements of fiction.

8. **justification** [jŭs tə fĭ kā´ shən] n. the act of showing or proving to be right

   The instructor gave me no <u>justification</u> for the F I got on my research paper.

9. **option** [ŏp´ shən] n. choice; the power or freedom to choose

   One <u>option</u> for the final exam is to give a fifteen-minute literary analysis of a poem.

10. **summary** [sûm´ ə rē] n. a brief statement mentioning the main points of something

    We each had to write a one-page <u>summary</u> of "The Lottery."

Vocabulary Practice with Word Forms

Now review this word form chart. Fill in the spaces with the correct form of the word from the Academic Word List. Use your dictionary if necessary to look up a word form.

NOUN	VERB	ADJECTIVE	ADVERB
_____	alternate	alternative	alternatively
X	X	_____	apparently
attitude	X	attitudinal	attitudinally
_____	contrast	contrasted, contrasting, contrastive	contrastively
criteria	X	X	X
_____	err	erroneous	erroneously
goals	X	X	X
_____	justify	justifiable, justified	justifiably
_____	opt	optional	optionally
_____	summarize	summarized	summarily

Discourse Markers

The following is a list of discourse markers you will hear in the extended lecture.

Discourse Marker	Function
At first glance	Introducing
If you ask me,	Giving an opinion
OK	Shifting subtopics
X is a type of Y	Defining
in terms of	Setting parameters

NOTE: For a complete list of discourse markers and commonly used expressions, see Appendix 2, page 129.

Listen and Respond

ACTIVITY 10

Listen to the Extended Lecture

First Listening: Listen for Discourse Markers You will hear an extended lecture played two times. The first time, listen to the discourse markers that organize the information. They are written below. Fill in the next two or three words following the discourse markers as you hear them.

1. At first glance, _____

2. If you ask me, _____

3. OK, let's review _____

4. Point of view is a type of perspective _____

5. In terms of the basics of literature, _____

Second Listening: Listen and Take Notes Listen to the extended lecture again. Take notes using one of the methods you learned about in Chapter 1. If you are comfortable using note-taking symbols, practice them in this activity.

Compare your notes with those of a partner. Do you both have the same information?

Answer Questions about the Extended Lecture

Use your notes from the lecture to answer these questions. You may want to read the questions, then listen to the lecture again before answering.

1. Write two examples of plot given in the lecture.

_____

_____

_____

2. Are readers usually surprised by story plots? _____ Why or why not?

_____

_____

_____

3. How is point of view connected to the person who is telling the story?

_____

_____

_____

4. Write a brief definition of a narrator of a story. _____

_____

_____

5. Give a brief explanation of *theme*. _____

_____

_____

_____

6. What is the homework assignment for the next class? _____

_____

_____

7. What are the three processes that all fictional narratives give to the reader?

_____

_____

_____

Think Critically: Analyze a Famous Fairy Tale

Perhaps one of the most well-known stories in the world is the story of *Cinderella*. Cinderella is a young woman living a terrible life with her stepmother and stepsisters.

NOTE: If you are unfamiliar with the story of Cinderella, feel free to choose another well-known story.

Based on the information you have learned from the lectures, answer the questions about the story. Finally, write the theme that the author tries to convey to readers.

1. Title: _Cinderella_

2. Setting (remember, setting can include time, place, duration, etc.):

   _____

   _____

   _____

   _____

3. Main characters: _____

   _____

   _____

4. Plot (short summary): _____

   _____

   _____

   _____

   _____

5. Narrator (circle one):   first person (Cinderella)   third person

6. Central theme of the story: _____

   _____

   _____

   _____

Interviewing

Conduct Interviews: Analyze People's Reading Habits

Interviewing is a valuable skill for gathering information. The effectiveness of an interview rests mainly on the quality of the questions you ask and on how well you record the answers.

Task

Create a list of six questions to ask a classmate about his or her reading habits. Use the strategies below to help you write your questions and conduct the interview. Then share three interview answers with the class.

Interviewing Strategies

1. Bring a notebook and pen to the interview.

2. Avoid asking YES or NO questions (Do you read only fiction?). This kind of question limits the information you receive. Instead, ask open-ended questions beginning with *what, who, where, why,* and *how* (Where do you study, and what do you like about that college?). These questions will encourage the person you are interviewing to give longer answers and provide you with more useful information.

3. If the person does not understand the question, restate it another way or give an example of how you would answer the question.

4. Be aware of your tone of voice. Do not make judgments about the person being interviewed. A question such as "Do you think Stephen King is an example of a literary genius?" is not appropriate. Rather, ask "What is your opinion of Stephen King's writing style?"

5. Make sure you leave enough space in your notes to write a complete answer.

SAMPLE INTERVIEW FORM

| Interviewer name: | Date: |

| Interviewee name: | Subject: |

How often do you read outside of class?

What is your favorite type of book to read?

Compare Book Reviews

This activity will help you see how people analyze books differently. First, choose a book or short story to review. Then, find at least three different reviews of the same story. (Hint: Try checking large bookstores on the Internet for reviews by professional critics and readers.)

Compare and contrast the information presented in the reviews. Look for information about plot summary, characters, and theme. Record your observations in the chart below. If a review is missing any element, write "not in review."

Title of book or short story: _____

Author: _____ Year Published: _____

REVIEWERS	PLOT SUMMARY	CHARACTERS	THEME	STAR RATING (how many stars?)
Reviewer 1:				
Reviewer 2:				
Reviewer 3:				

 For more activities and information, go to the *Key Concepts* 2 website at *elt.heinle.com/keyconcepts.*

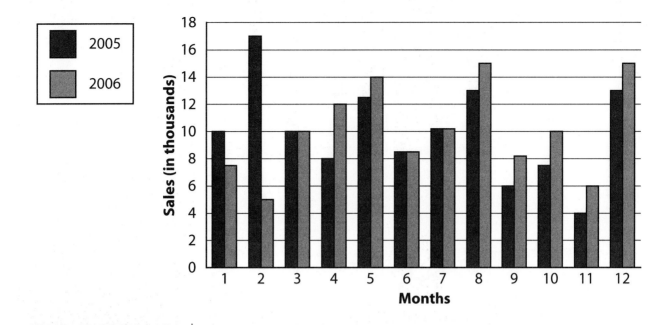

5 • From Mathematics: • Applied Mathematics

MAT 1330
Liberal Arts Mathematics I (3)

Liberal arts mathematics focuses on topics that will be helpful in developing a broader base of mathematical knowledge. Some of the topics covered in this course include: finite and infinite sets, probability, graph theory, voting theory, and reflections and translations in geometry.

Mathematics is a broad field of study divided into traditional math (algebra, calculus, etc.) and applied mathematics. When entering college, a lot of students are unaware that their major dictates the type of math they need to study. Only students who are interested in pursuing degrees in hard sciences such as engineering and physics need to study the traditional mathematical concepts. For many others, particularly those students interested in Liberal Arts, many courses are available that satisfy mathematics requirements. This chapter focuses on one of those courses, Liberal Arts Math (also referred to as Applied Math).

Read the description on the left of a math course for students working towards a liberal arts degree.

Now find a course description for an introductory mathematics course from your community college or university catalog. What similarities do the two courses have? What are the differences?

This chapter will help you understand some **key concepts** of applied mathematics, such as

• understanding the basics of graphs

• labeling the parts of a graph

• understanding formation of paths and circuits

You will also practice some academic skills for success.

Get Ready to Listen

ACTIVITY ❶ *Brainstorming and Discussion*

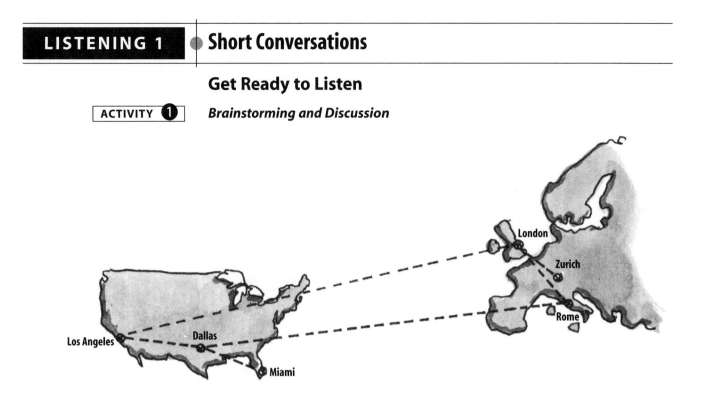

Look at the map as you answer these questions.

1. Your cousin who lives in Dallas wants to visit Rome. Look at the map above. What is the most direct route for your cousin to take? _____

   _____

2. Is this the only path she can take? _____ If not, describe an alternate path.

   _____

   _____

   _____

In mathematical terms, you have just created a *path*. Now, if your cousin's trip begins and ends in the same place (like most travelers who use round-trip tickets), this is called a *circuit*.

Listen and Respond

Listen to Conversations

Indivisible Phrasal Verbs

You learned in Chapter 1 that phrasal verbs are verb/preposition combinations. The list of phrasal verbs you will hear in the conversations are indivisible—they cannot be separated. As you listen, try to understand the meaning of the phrasal verbs based on the context of the conversation. Then circle the best answers below.

NOTE: For a complete list of phrasal verbs, see Appendix 3, page 132.

1. A person who is <u>called on</u> probably needs to
   a. say something out loud
   b. write something down
   c. leave the room
   d. answer the telephone

2. People who <u>go over</u> something
   a. know the information already
   b. want to review the information
   c. want to memorize information
   d. lead others in information gathering

3. After you <u>go through</u> supplies, you probably want to
   a. give your supplies to others
   b. stop using your supplies
   c. get new supplies
   d. start using different supplies

4. "Could you <u>look after</u> my _____?"
   a. glasses
   b. pets
   c. test
   d. honesty

5. <u>Look into</u> means
   a. watch
   b. memorize
   c. research
   d. inspect

6. If you <u>take after</u> someone, you
   a. come after that person
   b. resemble that person
   c. rob that person
   d. love that person

7. If someone <u>means to</u> do something, that action is probably
   a. funny
   b. intentional
   c. quick
   d. dangerous

ACTIVITY **3** | *Review Phrasal Verbs*

Choose four of the seven phrasal verbs from the conversations. Write a sentence using each phrasal verb. When you are finished, share your sentences with the rest of the class.

call on	go over	go through	mean to
look after	look into	take after	

1. _____
   _____

2. _____
   _____

3. _____
   _____

4. _____
   _____

LISTENING 2 ● Mini-Lecture: Graphs

Vocabulary

Academic Word List

Practice reading and saying aloud these vocabulary words. How many of the words do you already know?

1. **alter** [ôl´ tər] v. to make something different; change

   The instructor had to <u>alter</u> his plans for the test because of a family emergency.

2. **attribute** [ə trib´ yōōt´] v. to consider something as belonging to or resulting from something. n. [ăt´ rə byōōt´] quality or characteristic of belonging to or resulting from somebody or something; a quality or distinctive feature

   Many people <u>attribute</u> their success in math courses to their instructors. (v)
   One universal <u>attribute</u> of mathematicians is a curiosity about the order of the universe. (n)

3. **component** [kəm pō´ nənt] n. one of the parts that make up a whole

   <u>Components</u> such as vertices and lines make up a graph.

4. **considerable** [kən sĭd´ ər ə bəl] adj. much; a lot of

   The instructor gave <u>considerable</u> thought to the math word problems she gave on the test.

5. **correspond (with / to)** [kôr´ ĭ spŏnd´] or [kŏr ĭ spŏnd´] v. (… with) to be in agreement; (… to) to be similar or equivalent

   The final graph needs to <u>correspond</u> to its *x* and *y* coordinates.

6. **dominant** [dom´ ə nənt] adj. having the most influence or control

   Using a graphing calculator has had a <u>dominant</u> role in increasing students' success in mathematics classes.

7. **investigation** [ĭn vĕs tĭ gā´ shən] n. a careful examination or search in order to discover facts or gain information

   Upon <u>investigation</u>, it was discovered that Donny cheated on his Algebra final exam.

8. **obvious** [ob´ vē əs] adj. evident; easily seen or understood

   Students often fail to see the <u>obvious</u> connections between graphs and everyday life.

9. **predict** [prĭ dĭkt´] v. to tell about in advance; to foretell

   I would have never <u>predicted</u> that I would enjoy my liberal arts math class so much.

10. **series** [sîr´ ēz] n. (pl.) a number of similar things or events that follow one another

    A <u>series</u> of dots and lines constitutes a graph.

| ACTIVITY 4 | **Vocabulary Practice with Word Forms** |

Review this word form chart. Fill in the spaces with the correct form of the word from the Academic Word List. You may use a dictionary if you need help.

NOUN	VERB	ADJECTIVE	ADVERB
alteration	_____	altered	X
_____	attribute	attributed, attributive	attributively
component	X	componential	X
consideration	_____	considerable	considerably
correspondence	_____	corresponding, correspondent	correspondingly
domination	dominate	dominant	_____
investigation, investigator	_____	investigated, investigative	X
X	X	obvious	_____
prediction	_____	predicted, predictable	_____
series	X	X	X

Discourse Markers

Study the following discourse markers and their functions. You will hear these discourse markers in the mini-lecture.

Discourse Marker	Function
The purpose of this talk today is	Introducing
to begin with	Listing
By the way	Giving additional information
let me put it another way	Clarifying
furthermore	Emphasizing

NOTE: For a complete list of discourse markers and commonly used expressions, see Appendix 2, page 129.

Listen and Respond

Listen to the Mini-Lecture

First Listening: Listen for Vocabulary You will hear a mini-lecture played two times. The first time, listen for descriptions of graphs. Study the graphs below as you listen to the lecture.

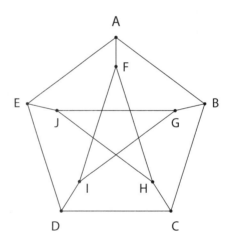

Diagram 1: The Petersen Graph

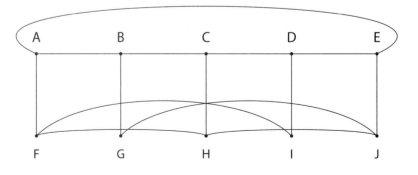

Diagram 2: Alternative Visual Representation of the Petersen Graph

Key Concepts 2: Listening, Note Taking, and Speaking Across the Disciplines

Second Listening: Listen and Take Notes Listen to the mini-lecture again. Take notes using one of the methods you learned about in Chapter 1. Remember that the content of a lecture is very important and will most likely appear on a test. For this reason, good note-takers focus on key content words and ideas rather writing down every word.

NOTE: If you use symbols instead of words to save time while taking notes, refer to Appendix 5 on page 139 for more information on using note-taking symbols.

Compare your notes with a partner's. Do you both have the same information?

Answer Questions about the Mini-Lecture

Use your notes from the lecture to answer these questions. You may want to read the questions, then listen to the lecture again before answering.

1. Define a graph. _____
   _____

2. Who was Petersen? _____
   _____

3. Why is the Petersen graph important? _____
   _____

4. What is a vertex? _____
   _____

5. Study the Petersen graph on page 79. How many vertices are found on this graph? _____ Write them out. _____

6. Define an edge. _____
   _____

7. Show 5 examples of edges on the Petersen graph. _____
   _____

LISTENING 3 ● Pronunciation

Modals *can* and *can't*

One of the most difficult distinctions for students to hear and pronounce is *can* and its negative *can't*. The modal *can*, when used in a statement, is generally pronounced with a reduced vowel. [k-ə-n].

In the negative form, however, the vowel is more open and pronounced [kăn]. Native speakers usually do not pronounce the final [t] in the word *can't*.

ACTIVITY 7

Listen for can and can't

Listen to the following sentences and circle the word you hear.

1. Dana (can / can't) do the problems without the calculator!

2. I don't think I (can / can't) pass this calculus class.

3. Dr. Bamfo (can / can't) have our midterm exams graded until we all return from Spring Break.

4. (Can / Can't) you grade them while you're on the plane?

5. Well, graphs (can / can't) be used to represent any number of things.

6. Graphs (can / can't) show the neighborhood locations of streets and houses.

7. A graph (can / can't) be useful to a post office in figuring out the most efficient way to deliver mail.

8. Like a path, in a circuit, an edge (can / can't) be traveled at most once.

LISTENING 4 ● Extended Lecture: Kinds of Graphs and Their Functions

Vocabulary

Academic Word List

Practice reading and saying aloud these vocabulary words. How many do you already know?

1. **code** [kōd] n. a system of words, symbols, or letters used in place of ordinary writing

   The letter code AB is an example of one of the lines on the Petersen graph.

2. **core** [kôr] n. the innermost part of something

   Mail delivery routes are established by a graph, the core of many city planning projects.

3. **location** [lō kā´ shən] n. a place where something is; a site

   We wanted to join the math study group, but we couldn't find the location.

4. **mechanism** [měk´ ə nĭz´ əm] n. the working parts of a machine; a system of parts that work together

   When my calculator broke, I took it apart to check if each mechanism was working properly.

5. **overall** [o´ vər ôl] adj. including everything; viewed as a whole

   Many students' overall impression of College Algebra is that it is not useful in everyday life.

6. **publish** [pŭb´ lĭsh] v. to print and offer for public distribution or sale

   Our algebra book was published almost 30 years ago.

7. **retain** (retention) [rĭ tān´] v. to keep possession of something

   The math instructor retained his job even though he kept using the same tests over twenty years.

8. **sequence** [sē´ kwəns] n. the following of one thing after another

   At City College, the math sequence for students is Intermediate Algebra, College Algebra, and then Applied Mathematics.

9. **statistics** [stə tĭs´ tĭks] n. a collection or set of numerical data

   Statistics show that many students in the United States come to college without college-level math skills.

10. **subsequent** [sŭb´ sĭ kwĕnt´] adj. following something else in time or order

    I didn't understand the math professor's first word problem, but I got it on his subsequent example.

ACTIVITY 8 · *Vocabulary Practice with Word Forms*

Write the word forms in the box in the correct part-of-speech columns below. Some words may be more than one part of speech. Use your dictionary if necessary.

publish	code	statistic	sequentially	location
retained	code/codify	publishing	codified	core
subsequent	mechanized	statistical	locate	sequential
mechanization	overall	published	retain	sequence
mechanize	statistically	subsequently		

NOUN	VERB	ADJECTIVE	ADVERB

ACTIVITY 9 · *More Practice with Word Forms*

Circle the best word for each sentence.

1. The (statistical / coded) analysis of the test scores showed surprising results.

2. If you look at the variables (overall / sequentially), you should see a pattern develop from beginning to end.

3. The professor wasn't able to (mechanize / locate) his grade book.

4. Many mathematicians believe that the (core / location) of applied mathematics is graph theory.

5. The introduction of the calculator into the classroom (mechanized / published) the steps in solving math problems.

Discourse Markers

Study the following discourse markers and their functions. You will hear these discourse markers in the extended lecture.

Discourse Marker	Function
As we know	Giving background information
Let me give you some specific examples	Giving examples
However	Giving contrasting information
We've seen that	Summarizing/concluding
To my mind	Giving opinion

NOTE: For a complete list of discourse markers and commonly used expressions, see Appendix 2, page 129.

Listen and Respond

ACTIVITY **10**

Listen to the Extended Lecture

First Listening: Listen for Specific Information You will hear a lecture played two times. The first time, note the uses of the discourse markers in the lecture. There are five. As you hear the discourse markers, prepare to write down some of the information that immediately follows them. Use the spaces provided for your answers.

1. **As we know**, a graph is _____ up of a series _____ dots and _____.

2. **Let me give you some specific examples**. _____ show the neighborhood _____ of streets and houses.

3. **However**, the following is _____ a path from A _____ E.

4. **We've seen that** _____ and circuits have _____ properties.

5. **To my mind**, these programs have _____ the way that mathematicians _____ their work.

Second Listening: Listen and Take Notes Listen to the extended lecture again. Take notes using one of the methods you learned about in Chapter 1. If you are comfortable using note-taking symbols, practice them in this activity.

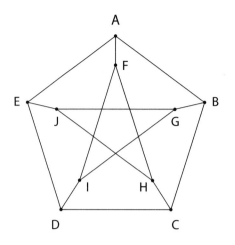

Compare your notes with a partner's. Discuss any information that is different.

Use your notes from the lecture to answer these questions. Read each multiple choice statement. Circle the letter of the best answer.

1. A graph is made up of a series of _____.
   a. points and dots
   b. dots and vertices
   c. dots and lines
   d. lines and codes

2. Graphs are often used by post offices to be more _____.
   a. modern
   b. mathematical
   c. complicated
   d. efficient

3. A / An _____ begins and ends at *different* vertices.
   a. circuit
   b. graph
   c. path
   d. edge

4. Study the Petersen graph. An example of a path from A to E is _____.
   a. ABGJE
   b. AEFJC
   c. DIFGB
   d. AEDCA

5. A *circuit* is a path that _____.
   a. is longer than a traditional circuit
   b. begins and ends at a different vertex
   c. begins and ends at the same vertex
   d. travels across the same vertex more than once

6. Study the Petersen graph. Which of the following is a correct circuit (from A to A)?
   a. ABCDEA
   b. AFIDA
   c. AFJDEA
   d. ABEA

7. A mail carrier stops his truck on the corner of a residential street. He needs to deliver mail (on foot) to twenty families. What method does he need to use in order to complete his deliveries here and go on to the next neighborhood?
   a. vertex
   b. path
   c. Petersen graph
   d. circuit

| ACTIVITY 12 | **Think Critically: Circuits and Paths** |

Review multiple-choice question 7 in Activity 11. Explain why your answer is the best choice for the mail carrier. _____

_____

Now think of 2 examples in everyday life where people would use a path system and a circuit system.

Path

1. _____

2. _____

Circuit

1. _____

2. _____

| **SPEAKING** | ● **Using Visual Aids** |

| ACTIVITY 13 | **Explain a Visual** |

Here you will give a presentation that explains a graph, table, model, diagram, or flow chart.

Task

Step 1: Choose a graph that you want to explain to the class. This visual does not have to be from math. It can be from a business magazine, a website, a textbook, or something you created yourself. The topic can range from sports to test scores. Try to find a topic that you are interested in. In your explanation use as many discourse markers and common phrases and expressions as you can.

Step 2: Share your graph with your teacher before you begin. If you cannot find a suitable graph, your teacher might be able to provide you with one.

Step 3: Decide how you are going to present your visual to the class. Will you distribute your visual as a handout, on an overhead (with either a transparency or a computer), or on the board?

Step 4: Practice discussing your graph alone or to friends before doing it in front of the class. Try to use discourse markers in your explanation. Refer to Appendix 2, page 129, for a list of discourse markers.

In your explanation, use as many discourse markers and common phrases and expressions as you can.

Guidelines

Do a graph analysis before you begin your explanation. Answer the following questions about the graph.

- Does the graph have a title or a name?
- What is the purpose of the graph?
- Are there any symbols or words that you need to explain to the class?
- Can you make any predictions about the graph?

What are the main points that you want to summarize about the graph as you end your presentation?

ACTIVITY ⑭

Describe a Circuit

In this activity, you will use your graph skills to explain a typical day at school.

Step 1: In the space provided, draw a simple map of your school. Try to include as many of the following structures:

parking lot	sports complex	cafeteria
library	dormitories	student services

You may add other structures, but try to include at least five structures in your map.

Step 2: Label each building in two ways: with the name of the building and with a corresponding letter. (i.e., A, B, C, etc.)

Step 3: Exchange your map with a partner.

Step 4: Choose one person to go first. Tell your partner what your route is on a typical day at school. For example, if you drive to school and go to the library before class, say, "I arrive at the parking lot. Then I go to the library. After about an hour, I go to class in the Humanities building. Then I grab a cup of coffee at the cafeteria."

Your partner will write down the information using circuit language.

Step 5: Now change roles.

 For more activities and information, go to the *Key Concepts* 2 website at *elt.heinle.com/keyconcepts*.

6 · From History: American History

History is the study of our past and a key to our understanding of who and what we are today. The course listing on the left fills one of the requirements for students interested in majoring in American history.

Find a course description for a similar introductory American history class in your community college or university catalog. What similarities do the two courses have? What are the differences?

This chapter will help you understand some **key concepts** of American history, such as.

- the role of historians
- reasons the Europeans first came to the Americas
- economic reasons for the migration westward in the United States
- "Manifest Destiny" and what part it played in American history
- the roles of Mexico, France, and Native Americans in defining the boundaries of the United States

You will also practice some academic skills for success.

HIS 1401
Conquest of the Americas (3)

When Europeans began their exploration of the Americas, it launched centuries of conflict. This course will examine this momentous historical period, from the initial contacts with indigenous Americans through the U.S. settlement of the American West, and analyze the repercussions of this conflict for both cultures.

Get Ready to Listen

Brainstorming and Discussion

Work in small groups to match these quotes about history and historians to the ideas in the sentences in column 2. Use your dictionary to help you with words you don't know.

1. _____ "God alone knows the future, but only an historian can alter the past." — Ambrose Bierce

2. _____ "To know the truth of history is to realize its ultimate myth and its inevitable ambiguity." — Roy P. Basler

3. _____ "History must be written of, by, and for the survivors." — Anonymous

4. _____ "If you would understand anything, observe its beginning and its development." — Aristotle

5. _____ "History is a myth that men agree to believe." — Napoleon

6. _____ "History is something that happens to other people." — Anonymous

7. _____ "It is the essence of the poor that they do not appear in history." — Anonymous

8. _____ "A country without a memory is a country of madmen." — George Santayana

a. People who have no knowledge about or interest in their past can do dangerous and stupid things.

b. History is written by the people who succeeded.

c. We need to understand the things that caused the big events in history, not just the events themselves.

d. History can't tell us what really happened.

e. We never think of ourselves as being part of history.

f. Historians have the power to change history.

g. History is just what people decide to believe.

h. History is written about the rich and powerful.

Now choose two quotes that you agree with and explain to your group why you agree with them. Try to think of examples to support your opinion.

Listen and Respond

Listen to Conversations

Listen to the sentences below. The missing words are the phrasal verbs listed in the box. Write the ones you hear in the appropriate blanks. You will need to change some of them to the third-person -s ending that you hear. Then read the definitions in the exercise that follows and write in the phrasal verb that you think matches each one.

put up with	do over	set off	get along
pile on	look back on	get through	

Bill: Hi Kerry, what did professor Truitt think about your report on the American Civil War?

Kerry: Not much. He said we had to _____ the whole first section about the causes of the war. I will be working on it all weekend.

Bill: What do you mean? Aren't you and June doing the report together?

Kerry: Well yeah, but so far I have done most of the work. And every time I ask her to help me she just _____ the excuses about how busy she is.

Bill: I wouldn't _____ that! You should tell her to do some of it.

Kerry: I've tried, but it just _____ a big argument between us.

Bill: Well, can you _____ it by yourself?

Kerry: I think so. But I am going to _____ this experience whenever she asks me for help in the future. It's a shame. She and I used to _____ very well. But this has changed my feelings about her.

1. finish _____
2. give a lot of _____
3. accept a situation or behavior that you don't like _____
4. have a good relationship _____
5. start again _____
6. cause to begin _____
7. review; look at or remember something from the past _____

Vocabulary

Academic Word List

Practice reading and saying aloud these vocabulary words. How many of the words do you already know?

1. **access** [ăk´ sĕs] n. the right to enter, reach, or use

   We have <u>access</u> to the teacher's history books for our research.

2. **approximate** [ə prŏk´ sə mĭt] adj. almost exact or accurate

   The <u>approximate</u> time of the last "Indian Wars" in American history was from the 1860s to the 1890s.

3. **debate** [dĭ bāt´] n. a discussion of the arguments for and against something

   We had a <u>debate</u> yesterday in history class about the rights of Native Americans.

4. **emphasis** [ĕm´ fə sĭs] n. special forcefulness of expression or effort that gives importance or focus

   Dr. Whetsel puts a lot of <u>emphasis</u> on understanding the reasons for historical events.

5. **implication** [ĭm´ plĭ kā´ shən] n. something expressed indirectly

   The <u>implications</u> of the U.S.'s desire to expand westward was the destruction of the Native American way of life.

6. **label** [lā´ bəl] v. to identify and classify n. a descriptive word or phrase used to identify or describe

   The teacher asked us to <u>label</u> the different political movements in post-revolutionary America. (v)
   "Liberal" and "conservative" are <u>labels</u> to define people's political points of view. (n)

7. **link** [lĭngk] n. something that joins or connects

   Native Americans felt a close <u>link</u> with nature.

8. **maximum** [măk´ sə məm] adj. relating to the greatest or most possible or permitted

   The teacher gave us the <u>maximum</u> amount of time we have for our research paper on the American Revolution.

9. **resolution** [rĕz´ ə lōō´ shən] n. a decision to do something with firm determination; an answer or explanation

   President Lincoln made a <u>resolution</u> to end slavery.
   Moving westward was the <u>resolution</u> to the early U.S. population problem.

10. **validity** [və lĭd´ ĭ tē] n. the quality of being logical, legal, or convincing

    Our professor questioned the <u>validity</u> of the purchase of land from the Native Americans.

ACTIVITY 3   *Vocabulary Practice*

Some of the words in the Academic Word List can be used in other parts of speech, in different forms or the same forms, without changing their basic meaning. Complete the sentences with words from the box. Write the part of speech in the blanks at the end of the sentences. Use these abbreviations: noun = n, verb = v. The first one is done for you.

~~debate~~	label	implicate	link	maximum	access

1. I'm sorry, but we can't ____*debate*____ this issue any longer. We have to make a decision. __v__

2. Your oral reports should be a _____ of ten minutes. Please make sure they are no longer than that. _____

3. When the police questioned him, he refused to _____ his friends in the crime. _____

4. We should try not to put a _____ on people. Everyone is different. _____

5. I can't _____ that information right now because the electricity has gone out. I'll have to try again later. _____

6. Historians try to _____ ideas and events of a period in history in order to better understand them. _____

ACTIVITY 4   *Vocabulary Practice with Word Forms*

Look at the different forms of some of the Academic Word List words in the box below. Use the three forms of the same word in the appropriate group of sentences that follows.

Verb	Adjective	Adverb
emphasize	emphatic	emphatically
approximate	approximate	approximately
resolve	resolute	resolutely

1. I really don't know how to _____ this problem. She disagrees _____ with me. I guess we should just be _____ in continuing to try to reach an agreement.

2. I want to _____ that all of your reports must be done by Friday. The reason I say this _____ is that I want to read them over the weekend and return them to you for discussion on Monday. I am _____ about this, so please don't hand them in late.

3. *Student*: Can you _____ the time we will have for our class presentations?

   Teacher: They should be _____ ten minutes long.

   Student: Mine will go a few minutes longer than the _____ time. Is that okay?

Discourse Markers and Commonly Used Expressions

The words below are discourse markers and commonly used expressions. You will hear them in the mini-lecture.

Discourse Marker	Function
in this respect	Clarify
in addition	Give further information
parenthetically speaking	Clarify
lest we forget	Emphasize

Commonly Used Expressions		
A point of contention	back and forth	hardly the case

NOTE: You will see the functions of these phrases in Activity 5. For a complete list of discourse markers and commonly used expressions, see Appendix 2, page 129.

 ACTIVITY 5

Sequence Statements and Match Definitions

These statements about the travel westward in the 19th century are out of order. Number them in the correct order. Then look in the sentences for the discourse markers and commonly used phrases in the lists above. Match them with their meanings in the box. Write the meanings above the underlined words.

in case we don't remember	by the way	
an issue of strong disagreement	not the situation	go and return
relating to this	~~also~~	

 1. But <u>lest we forget</u>, up until the invention of trains, planes, and cars, this was <u>hardly the case</u>.

2. After a few years in the U.S., many of them missed their homelands across the oceans too much and made the difficult voyage back to the life they had known before.

3. However, of the millions of people who moved westward, some ended up not liking their new lives in the West and made the difficult journey back East.

4. Nowadays it is easy to <u>go back and forth</u> quickly across the continental United States.

5. <u>In this respect</u>, such moves often meant leaving one's friends and neighbors forever.

1 6. Good morning class. Today I'd like to talk about the migration of U.S. citizens from the East to the West of America in the first half of the 19th century.

7. <u>Parenthetically speaking</u>, this was also true of immigrants who came to America from other countries.

also
8. <u>In addition</u>, if the move was <u>a point of contention</u> among family members, it could even mean the permanent separation of these members.

9. Before these inventions, a trip westward in the U.S. typically took a year or more and was filled with dangers, so a return trip was not usually something people did.

Listen and Respond

ACTIVITY 6

Listen to the Mini-Lecture

First Listening: Listen for Vocabulary You will hear a mini-lecture played two times. The first time, listen for vocabulary from the Academic Word List. Fill in the vocabulary words you hear below.

1. ... applying the _____ of peace-loving ...

2. ... the _____ of this course ...

3. ... happened and its _____ for American history ...

4. ... I will give a _____ amount of time ...

5. ... the _____ of this claim ...

6. ... a long-standing _____ ...

7. ... around the _____ time as those ...

8. ... resulted in the European _____ to find ...

9. ... an easier _____ for _____ to trade ...

Second Listening: Listen and Take Notes Listen to the mini-lecture again. Take notes using one of the note-taking methods you learned about in Chapter 1.

Compare your notes with those of a partner. Discuss any information that is different.

ACTIVITY 7   *Answer Questions about the Mini-Lecture*

Use your notes from the lecture to answer these questions. You may want to read the questions, then listen to the lecture again before answering.

1. The teacher says that the history he will teach the class is written by the people who lost the conflict between the Europeans and Native Americans.   TRUE   FALSE

2. The teacher believes that it is generally agreed that the Native Americans were not treated fairly.   TRUE   FALSE

3. What label does he think is not accurate for all the Native Americans of that time period?

    _____

4. The teacher says he doesn't want to go "back and forth" on the issue of violence between Europeans and Native Americans. This means he:
    a. doesn't want to talk about Europeans and Native Americans.
    b. wants to talk about injustice to the Europeans.
    c. doesn't want to spend a lot of time arguing about this point in class.

5. What will he emphasize in the class?

    _____

    _____

6. What will the teacher spend the maximum amount of time on in the class?

    _____

    _____

7. What is the disagreement over Christopher Columbus between Italy and Spain?

    _____

    _____

8. Why are Native Americans called Indians?

    _____

    _____

9. What is Amerigo Vespucci famous for?

    _____

10. Why did the Europeans look for an easier link to trade with India?

    _____

Vowel and Syllable Length in Stress and Pitch

English has many words whose vowel length is determined by the consonant that comes right after the vowel.

ACTIVITY 8

Listen for Vowel Length

Listen to the following sentences and circle the underlined word that has a longer /i/ sound.

> **What time does the sun rise?**
> **Are we having rice for dinner?**

As you heard, "rise" has a longer /i/ sound than "rice".

A. Look at the pairs of words below. Say them to yourself and circle the word you think has the longer vowel. Then listen to the recording. Were your choices correct?

1. belief	believe	5. face	faze	9. sent	send
2. give	gift	6. bead	beat	10. light	lied
3. road	wrote	7. wives	wife	11. root	rude
4. home	hope	8. need	neat	12. coat	code

RULE: Voiced consonants make the vowel sound longer, and unvoiced consonants make the vowel sound shorter.

How do you know which is which? Unvoiced sounds have no vibration in your throat and usually have more breath afterwards (example: the "f" in belief).

B. Pronounce the <u>sound</u> (not the name) of the following letters. Put a V for voiced or U for unvoiced next to each one.

M _____	P _____	B _____	N _____
D _____	T _____	K _____	G _____
L _____	V _____	F _____	R _____
Z _____	S _____		

Now listen to the recording and see if your answers are correct.

C. Some of the sounds of the letters you have just pronounced have the exact same lip and tongue placement in your mouth, for example P and B. The only difference is the unvoiced sound in P and the voiced sound in B. In the list in B above, circle P and B. Now circle the other pairs of sounds that have only the unvoiced/voiced difference. There are four more pairs (they are next to each other.)

D. Now get with a partner and read one of the words in the pairs below. Remember the sounds of the consonants you did in Part B. Student A reads 1–6 and Student B marks the words he or she hears with either V (voiced) or U (unvoiced). Then Student B reads 7–12 and Student A marks the words he or she hears with either V or U.

STUDENT A				STUDENT B			
1. ___ belief	___ believe			7. ___ need	___ neat		
2. ___ home	___ hope			8. ___ root	___ rude		
3. ___ wives	___ wife			9. ___ road	___ wrote		
4. ___ light	___ lied			10. ___ bead	___ beat		
5. ___ give	___ gift			11. ___ sent	___ send		
6. ___ face	___ faze			12. ___ coat	___ code		

Did your partner mark the words you said?

ACTIVITY 9

Listen for Syllable Length and Pitch

Vowel sounds in stressed syllables are also made longer and the pitch (sound) goes up. For example, in the word "decide" the syllable "cide" is stressed and longer than the syllable "de", and the pitch is higher. In the word "university", the syllable "ver" is stressed and longer and pitched higher than the other syllables.

The following words are from the mini-lecture. They have been divided into syllables. Work with a partner and underline the syllables you think are stressed and have a longer sound and a higher pitch. Practice saying these words with a partner and then listen to the recording to see if your pronunciation was accurate.

his <u>tor</u> i cal	con ten tion	de bate
Na tive A mer icans	par en thet i cal ly speak ing	ap prox i mate
ap plies	em pha sis	res o lu tion
cul ture	im pli ca tions	ac cess
bru ta li ty	max i mum	
in jus tices	va lid i ty	

Vocabulary

Academic Word List

Practice reading and saying aloud these vocabulary words. How many do you already know?

1. **civil** [sĭv´ əl] adj. relating to citizens and their rights and status; polite

    Our civil rights are written into the U.S. Constitution.
    If you can't be civil to me, please don't talk to me.

2. **conference** [kŏn´ fər əns] or [kŏn´ frəns] n. a meeting, sometimes regional and public, to discuss a subject or a number of subjects

    A big conference of historians met in town this week.

3. **consent** [kən sĕnt´] n. agreement and acceptance; permission

    Queen Isabela gave her consent to Christopher Columbus's request for money to find a new sea route to India.

4. **exclude** [ĭk sklood´] v. to prevent from entering; to not include

    The government excluded some of the information from the report.

5. **imply** [ĭm plī´] v. to say or express indirectly

    The look on the teacher's face implied she was not satisfied with the students' understanding of the lecture.

6. **layer** [lā´ ər] n. a single thickness of material lying between others or covering a surface

    A lot of history can be learned by examining the layers of earth at sites where cities once existed.

7. **philosophy** [fĭ lŏs´ ə fē] n. the study of or manner of thinking by logical reasoning of such things as the universe, nature, life, morals; a general point of view

    Native Americans had a very different philosophy from Europeans about the relationship between humans and the Earth.

8. **prior** [prī´ ər] adj., adv. coming before in time, order, or importance

    Explorations of America may have been done prior to Columbus by the Scandinavians.

9. **regime** [rā zhēm´] or [rĭ zhēm´] n. a government or system of government; a system of care or treatment

    The regime in that country was changed after the war.
    I'm getting fat. I need to get into an exercise regime.

10. **scheme** [skēm] n. a secret plan or plot; an orderly combination or arrangement

    The scheme to overthrow the government failed.
    In Native American art, the color schemes are often very bright.

 **ACTIVITY 10**

Vocabulary Practice

Read the following announcement and fill in the blanks with the words below from the Academic Word List.

> consent   imply   scheme   prior   philosophy   conference   civil   exclude

Welcome to our _____ on U.S. westward expansion in the 1800's. First, let's go over the list of presenters. As you can see on the schedule, there are speakers with many different points of view here. The _____ of the organizers of this conference is that we should not _____ any opinions, as perhaps you can see by the debate tomorrow night entitled "The Settlement of the American West: Idealistic Plan or Land-Grab _____?" We know that this is an emotional subject for many of you, and I don't mean to _____ that we expect impolite behavior, but let me just say that during the debate all attendees will try to be _____ to one another. On the last day of the conference and _____ to the closing session, there will be an excursion to the nearby Native American Navajo Reservation where the elders of the tribe have given their _____ for us to observe a tribal marriage ceremony. We hope you enjoy your time at the conference, and if you have any questions, our people at the Information Booth will be happy to help you.

ACTIVITY 11

Unscramble and Use Word Forms

A. Below are the scrambled letters of different parts of speech of some of the words from the Academic Word List. Most of them have different spellings, a few keep the same spelling, and two of them are only used in the part of speech from the word list. Unscramble these words and write them in the blanks. The first letters are given to you.

Nouns		**Verbs**	
ilivicyt	_civility_	fernoc	c
ticamlipnoi	i	lipzephosohi	p
cuxelnios	e	tenoscn	c
mireeg	r	shmeec	s

Adjectives		**Adverb**	
yeldare	l	ripor	p

B. Now use the words you have unscrambled to complete these sentences.

1. You shouldn't be so rude. Please try to show more _civility_ to me.

2. The _____ in power in that country does not respect human rights.

3. She likes to _____ about the important questions in life.

4. I like the _____ style of your new hair cut. It makes your hair look fuller.

5. Don't _____ against the boss. If he finds out about it, he'll fire you.

6. Her _____ from the party's guest list made her angry.

7. My father won't _____ to my missing school for a semester to travel.

8. He didn't say anything, but his smile was a/an _____ that he liked our idea.

9. Let's all get together and _____ on this problem.

10. He worked for a year _____ to entering the university.

ACTIVITY ⑫ **Work with Discourse Markers and Phrases**

In the statements below, read the underlined discourse markers and phrases that you will hear in the extended lecture. From the list in the box, write the meanings above the underlined words. The first one is done for you.

if	even more	find something wrong with
etcetera	basically	at the beginning
not for any reasons	with two opposing points of view or actions	
the truth is	~~it really isn't important~~	

it really isn't important
1. No matter what you say about him, I still think he is very nice.

2. We are working at cross purposes. I'm trying to save money for the future and you're spending it on things you think we need now.

3. I'll lend you the money you need on the condition that I can borrow your car this Friday.

4. What she says makes a lot of sense. I can't poke holes in any of it.

5. I enjoyed the party. There was lots of food, music, dancing, games, and so on.

6. The professor had many negative things to say about the regime in Washington during that period. <u>In a nutshell</u>, she thought it was not very effective and did not resolve the important issues of the time.

7. <u>At the onset</u> of the ceremony, everyone stood and sang the national anthem.

8. The job I'm being offered pays well, and the long vacation time makes it <u>all the more</u> desirable for me to take it.

9. <u>Under no circumstances</u> can you leave your seat while the plane is taking off.

10. I'd love to go to Europe on vacation this summer, but <u>when it comes down to it</u>, I just don't have enough money.

Listen and Respond

ACTIVITY **13**

Listen to the Extended Lecture

First Listening: Listen for Vocabulary
You will hear an extended lecture played two times. The first time, listen for vocabulary from the Academic Word List and fill in the blanks. You will hear the words in the order of the items here.

1. … came together in the _____ of "Manifest Destiny" …
2. … it was just a _____ to get the land …
3. … remove all the _____ of reasons that any political _____ might pile on …
4. … new liberties and _____ principles …
5. … with more states _____ that their own political power …
6. … did not give their _____, and this set off …
7. … pushed off their land and _____ from returning to it …
8. … Now, _____ to giving you your reading assignment …
9. … to tell you about a _____ at the university …

Second Listening: Listen and Take Notes Listen to the extended lecture again. Take notes using one of the methods you learned about in Chapter 1.

Compare your notes with those of a partner. Discuss any information that is different.

ACTIVITY **14**   *Answer Questions about the Extended Lecture*

Use your notes from the lecture to answer these questions. You may want to read the questions, then listen to the lecture again before answering.

1. What did John O'Sullivan mean by the term "Manifest Destiny"?

   _____

2. The population of the United States in the mid-19th century was
   _____ higher than in it was in 1800.
   a. almost five times
   b. less than four times
   c. five times

3. What land was included in the Louisiana Purchase and from whom did we buy the land?

   _____

   _____

4. Why was it necessary for the citizens in the eastern part of the U.S. to move westward? What reason made such a move all the more desirable?

_____

_____

5. Explain the philosophy of Manifest Destiny.

_____

_____

6. What were two reasons that some Americans opposed Manifest Destiny?

_____

_____

7. What two groups owned or lived on the land that the United States wanted?

_____

8. What area of the U.S. was taken from Mexico as a result of the Mexican-American War?

_____

ACTIVITY ⓰   *Think Critically: Roles in History*

Below is a list of things or people from the lecture. All of them played a favorable or unfavorable role in the movement for Manifest Destiny. Without using your notes, put F (favorable) or U (unfavorable) in the blanks next to the items and explain the role that each one had.

1. U.S. population growth _____   Role: _____

_____

2. Louisiana Purchase _____   Role: _____

_____

3. The abolitionists _____   Role: _____

_____

4. Mexico _____   Role: _____

_____

5. The Native Americans _____   Role: _____

_____

_____

 **ACTIVITY 16**

Participate in a Debate: Modern Native Americans

In a debate, people with opposing points of view discuss and argue their opinions for and against an issue.

Task

In this activity, you and your classmates will participate in an informal debate. The conflict between Native Americans and the U.S. Government in the 19th century continues to have consequences today for Native Americans. You will explore different Native American issues to debate. In your debate use as many discourse markers and common phrases and expressions as you can.

Strategies for Debate

Do the following for each of the debate topics on page 108:

1. Choose a controversy.

2. Choose one person to serve as the mediator of the debate. A mediator's job is to make sure that the groups are following the time limits and to maintain order.

3. Get together in a group that shares the same opinion, yes or no, about the issue. This is your debate team.

4. Compare your ideas with the other members of your debate team. On separate paper, make a list of the three best reasons that support your argument.

5. Choose one member to present the group's opinions and supporting reasons. Each group will have three minutes for this presentation.

6. While you listen to the group that has the opposing opinion, take notes about what they say. Each group will be given two minutes to organize a rebuttal (reply to the other group's points) when they are finished.

7. Choose a different person from your group to give a rebuttal in two minutes.

8. Open the discussion to anyone in either group to respond again to the arguments of the opposing group.

9. Use some of the·discourse markers, expressions, and vocabulary from this unit in your presentations.

Sample Debate Sequence

Group 1: YES (three-minute limit)

A. Introduce the topic and opinion

> **Be it resolved that Native Americans living on reservations should have their own laws and not be subject to the laws of the United States.**

B. Give supporting reasons for opinion

> **"There are many reasons, but the main ones are …"**

C. Give a concluding statement

> **"We urge you to support our position because …"**

Group 2: NO (three-minute limit)

A. Give opinions and supporting reasons

B. Give a concluding statement

Group 1:

A. Organize rebuttal privately (two-minute limit)

B. Present rebuttal (two-minute limit)

> **"We respectfully disagree with Group 2's opinion that …"**

C. Offer reasons why Group 2's ideas are wrong

> **"Group 2' s ideas are illogical because … "**

Group 2:

A. Organize rebuttal privately (two-minute limit)

B. Present rebuttal (two-minute limit)

Groups 1 and 2 (five-minute limit):

The floor is open to individuals from both groups to give their opinions.

Mediator (two-minute limit):

Make a decision and declare the winner of the debate.

Suggested Debate Topics

1. Reservations are lands given to Native Americans to live on by the U.S. government, but the reservations are subject to the federal and sometimes state laws of the United States.

   Debate: **Be it resolved that Native Americans living on reservations should have their own laws and not be subject to the laws of the United States.**

2. Native American reservations pay no taxes to the government, but the government provides them with services. Some of these reservations make millions of dollars from gambling casinos patronized by American taxpayers.

   Debate: **Be it resolved that Native American businesses on reservations should pay taxes to the United States government.**

3. The history and point of view of Native Americans is rarely mentioned in U.S. public school history classes. Many Native Americans are citizens of the United States and go to U.S. public schools.

   Debate: **Be it resolved that a course in Native American history should be required in the U.S. public school history curricula.**

 ACTIVITY ⓱   *Make a Poster about a Native American*

American history is full of famous Native Americans. With a partner, research one name from the list below. Make a poster that shows who the person was and what part he or she played in American history. If possible, include a quote from the person as well as a photo or drawing. Then display your poster so other students can read it and ask you questions about it.

Sitting Bull	Chief Joseph	Tecumseh	Pocahontas
Sacajawea	Black Hawk	Geronimo	Black Elk
Sequoyah	Osceola	Pontiac	

For more activities and information, go to the *Key Concepts* 2 website at *elt.heinle.com/keyconcepts*.

*A co-requisite is a course that needs to be taken simultaneously with another course.

Sir Isaac Newton (1642 – 1727)
English scientist known for his research in physics

7 From the Physical Sciences: Physics

Physics is the study of nature or natural objects. Whatever the name of the specific college course, from physics to natural philosophy to physical science, chances are that the course outline will include the laws and properties of matter and the forces acting upon it. Physics is concerned with the causes — such as heat, light, and motion — that change the general properties of objects.

Many physicists believe that physics is the only fundamental science. Because physics describes the internal configurations of atoms, and all matter is composed of atoms, other sciences could not exist without physics.

Read the description above of a required course for all science and engineering majors. Now find a course description for an introductory physics course from your community college or university catalog. What similarities do the two courses have? What are the differences?

This chapter will help you understand some **key concepts** of physics, such as

• Galileo's theories

• Sir Isaac Newton's contributions

• The First Law of Motion

You will also practice some academic skills for success.

LISTENING 1 ● Short Conversations

Get Ready to Listen

ACTIVITY **1**

Brainstorming and Discussion

Look at the picture of the Leaning Tower of Pisa. With a partner, answer the following questions.

1. Why do you think the tower is leaning?

   _____

   _____

2. With your partner, try to think of as many strategies as you can to straighten the tower. Be creative.

   _____

   _____

   _____

Listen and Respond

Three-Part Phrasal Verbs

You have learned that phrasal verbs are a combination of verb + preposition (particle). Some phrasal verbs actually contain three parts. In the following conversations, you will hear speakers use three-part phrasal verbs. Try to understand the meaning of the phrasal verbs based on the context of the conversation.

NOTE: Three-part phrasal verbs are not separable; that is, pronouns cannot be placed between the phrasal verb parts.

ACTIVITY **2**

Listen to Conversations

Now listen to the short conversations and circle the answers that give the meaning for the expressions you hear.

1. The phrase "catch up with" is connected to
   a. location
   b. time
   c. money
   d. intelligence

2. To "come up with" is related to finding the solution to something.   TRUE   FALSE

3. "Drop out of" is
   a. a positive thing
   b. a neutral thing
   c. a negative thing
   d. beyond a person's control

4. The phrase "keep up with" is the same as "catch up with."   TRUE   FALSE

5. In this sentence, the students need to "look out for" something
    a. bad
    b. good
    c. common
    d. fun

6. In this sentence, "talk out of" means
    a. speak too much
    b. convince someone to do something
    c. convince someone not to do something
    d. talk outdoors

7. If you "run out of" something, you should
    a. get more exercise
    b. wear comfortable shoes
    c. buy or get more
    d. continue doing what you were doing

Review Phrasal Verbs

Work with a partner. Choose three of the phrasal verbs in the box. Write a short conversation of at least 5 lines using the phrasal verbs. When you are finished, share your conversation with the rest of the class.

catch up with	come up with	drop out of	keep up with
look out for	run out of	talk … out of	

Speaker A: _____

_____

Speaker B: _____

_____

Speaker A: _____

_____

Speaker B: _____

_____

Speaker A: _____

_____

Vocabulary

Academic Word List

Practice reading and saying aloud these vocabulary words. How many of the words do you already know?

1. **adequate** [ăd´ ĭ kwĭt] adj. as much as is needed for a particular purpose; enough

   We don't have <u>adequate</u> time to finish our physics experiment today.

2. **constant** [kŏn´ stənt] adj. not changing. n. something that never changes

   An electric motor maintains a <u>constant</u> speed. (adj)
   When you are trying to figure out inertia, mass is a <u>constant</u>. (n)

3. **demonstrate** [dĕm´ ən strāt´] v. to show something clearly and deliberately

   Our professor <u>demonstrated</u> the law of motion yesterday by using some marbles.

4. **ensure** [ĕn shoor´] v. to make something sure or certain; to guarantee

   I need to <u>ensure</u> that I got the right notes from Dr. Laughlin.

5. **hypothesis** [hī pŏth´ ĭ sĭs] n. a statement that appears to explain a set of facts; a theory

   If a <u>hypothesis</u> is proved true, it becomes an accepted fact.

6. **physical** [fĭz´ ĭ kəl] adj. relating to the body rather than the mind or emotions; solid; material

   There is no doubting the <u>physical</u> proof of some of the experiments we are doing in lab class.

7. **project** [prŏj´ ĕkt´] n. a plan or proposal for a specific task. [prə jĕkt´] v. to push something forward or outward; to calculate or predict something in the future based on present information

   Our final <u>project</u> in physics class is to recreate Newton's first law. (n)
   Sometimes we can <u>project</u> the results of physics experiments before we complete them. (v)

8. **promote** [prə mōt´] v. to raise to a higher rank, position, or class; to aid the progress or growth of something

   Many of Aristotle's scientific ideas were wrongly <u>promoted</u> for thousands of years.

9. **reaction** [rē ăk´ shən] n. a response to something; a change

   The mixing of the two chemicals caused a major <u>reaction</u>.

10. **undertake** [ŭn´ dər tāk´] v. to decide or agree to do

    I didn't want to <u>undertake</u> the responsibility of being the main note taker during lab, but I have the neatest handwriting.

ACTIVITY 4 **Vocabulary Practice with Word Forms**

Complete each sentence with the correct form of the word in parentheses. Choose words ending from the box. Note that not every word needs an ending. Then write the part of speech.

NOTE: Some of the word forms you use might drop the final vowel.

-ing	-ly	-ion	-ize	-s	-ed	-d

1. Setting up yesterday's experiment was a huge (undertake) _____.

   Part of speech: _____

2. The assistant professor didn't get the (promote) _____ she was hoping for.

   Part of speech: _____

3. If Sir Isaac Newton hadn't (hypothesize) _____ about force and motion, how long would it have taken to understand the laws of motion?

   Part of speech: _____

4. In order to (demonstrate) _____ understanding of the theory, we have to complete a lab experiment.

   Part of speech: _____

5. I didn't study (adequate) _____ for the test, so I'm afraid my grade won't be very good.

   Part of speech: _____

6. I am (constant) _____ in the library. I never get to see the sun.

   Part of speech: _____

7. We couldn't (ensure) _____ the integrity of the experiment because our timepiece was not calibrated.

   Part of speech: _____

8. The (physical) _____ properties of those rock formations are consistent with our textbook's explanation.

   Part of speech: _____

9. The lab assistant was working on three separate (project) _____, so she didn't get a chance to validate the professor's experiment.

   Part of speech: _____

10. No one (react) _____ when the final exam grades were posted in the hallway.

    Part of speech: _____

Discourse Markers

Study the following discourse markers and their functions. You will hear these discourse markers in the mini-lecture.

Discourse Marker	Function
Today we're going to discuss	Introducing
X is actually	Defining
We should bear in mind that	Emphasizing
According to	Giving opinion (or source)

NOTE: For a complete list of discourse markers, see Appendix 2, page 129.

Listen and Respond

ACTIVITY 5

Listen to the Mini-Lecture

First Listening: Listen for Vocabulary You will hear a mini-lecture played two times. The first time, listen for the discourse markers. Then fill in the blanks with the words that follow the discourse markers.

1. Today we're going to discuss the history behind this _____ phenomenon.

2. In this case, _____ net reaction is actually equivalent _____ zero.

3. According to Isaac Newton's first _____ of motion, an object will _____ at rest...

4. We should bear in mind that Sir Isaac Newton was _____ in the same _____ that Galileo died.

Second Listening: Listen and Take Notes Listen to the mini-lecture again. Take notes using one of the methods you learned about in Chapter 1.

NOTE: If you use symbols to save time while taking notes, refer to Appendix 5 on page 139 for more information on using note-taking symbols.

Compare your notes with those of a partner. Do you both have the same information?

ACTIVITY **6**   *Answer Questions about the Mini-Lecture*

Use your notes from the lecture to answer these questions. You may want to read the questions, then listen to the lecture again before answering.

1. The lecturer describes force and motion as _____ and effect.

2. Force cannot change velocity.   TRUE   FALSE

3. One force can cancel or balance out another force.   TRUE   FALSE

4. Isaac Newton had a great influence on the ideas of
   Galileo.   TRUE   FALSE

5. The philosopher who developed ideas about motion
   more than 2000 years ago was _____.

6. An early hypothesis stated that the natural state of objects
   was to remain (circle one) at rest / moving.

7. Sir Isaac Newton studied objects in space.   TRUE   FALSE

8. Fill in the table with the correct information.

ORDER IN LECTURE	SCIENTIST NAME	THEORY
1st scientist		
2nd scientist		
3rd scientist		

Modal Auxiliaries

In the English language, modal auxiliary verbs are used to give additional meaning to the main verb. It is important to listen for modals and understand their meanings. Study the following examples:

Pronunciation note:

Younes will do his homework tomorrow.   often pronounced as an [l]

Younes would do his homework tomorrow.   often pronounced as a [d]

In the first sentence, **will** means that the homework is going to be completed. In the second sentence, **would** implies a condition. Younes will probably not do his homework.

Here is a list of commonly used modal auxiliaries:

may	might	could	would
be supposed to	have got to	must	have to
ought to	had better	can	be able to
will	be going to	shall	should

ACTIVITY ⑦

Listen for Modal Auxiliaries

As you listen to the statements from the mini-lecture, fill in the modal auxiliary you hear.

1. You _____ say that a push causes something to move.

2. This section of the course _____ discuss force and motion.

3. How_____ force be defined?

4. A force _____ act on an object.

5. … but its ability to ensure a change in motion _____ be canceled …

6. According to Isaac Newton's first law of motion, an object _____ remain at rest or in uniform motion in a straight line unless it is acted on by an external, unbalanced force.

7. He went on to hypothesize that if he _____ make a very long surface perfectly smooth, there would be nothing to stop the ball.

Vocabulary

Academic Word List

Practice reading and saying aloud these vocabulary words. How many do you already know?

1. **adjust(ed)** [ə jŭst´ ĭd] v. change, set, or regulate in order to improve something. adj. regulated or changed

   Raul adjusted the calculations to show that the acceleration of the car was faster than the motorcycle. (v)
   Our adjusted calculation showed that the acceleration of the car was faster than the motorcycle. (adj)

2. **concentration** [kŏn´ sən trā´ shən] n. the act of giving close attention; a close gathering or dense grouping

   Because of all the noise in the lecture hall, the speaker lost her concentration.

3. **constraint** [kən strānt´] n. something that restricts or prevents, as by the threat or use of force; a limitation

   There are obvious constraints on many of our experiments because we must stay in the classroom.

4. **internal** [ĭn tûr´ nəl] adj. located within the limits of or inside something; inner; interior

   The laws of physics, while mostly fascinating only to those with an internal interest in science, affect our everyday lives.

5. **parallel** [păr´ ə lĕl´] n. a comparison showing close resemblance. adj. with corresponding points always separated by the same distance. v. to be similar to something else

   When one studies Copernicus's and Galileo's experiments, one can easily see the parallels in their scientific thinking. (n)
   Although they lived in different times, many scientists believe that Galileo and Newton lived parallel lives. (adj)
   The discoveries made by Newton certainly parallel other discoveries of his time. (v)

6. **proportion** [prə pôr´ shən] n. the size, amount, or extent of one thing compared with another. v. to adjust something in order to reach a particular relation between parts

   Our results were out of proportion to the rest of the class's findings. (n)
   We didn't proportion the chemicals correctly before the experiment. (v)

7. **stress** [strĕs] n. importance or emphasis placed on something; a state of extreme difficulty, pressure, or strain. v. to cause somebody or something to feel physical or mental pressure or strain; to emphasize

   My level of stress got a lot lower after the mid-term exam. (n)
   Dr. Horvath stressed that we all take careful notes during the lab. (v)

8. **technical** [tĕk´ nĭ kəl] adj. relating to or derived from technique; relating to the practical, mechanical, or industrial arts or the applied sciences

   After explaining some of Newton's Laws, the professor got into more technical language that I didn't understand.

9. **technology** [tĕk nŏl´ ə jē] n. the use of scientific knowledge to solve practical problems

   Modern technology has simplified the way we gather information.

10. **volume** [vol´ yo͞om] or [vŏl´ yəm] n. quantity or amount; the amount of space occupied by a three-dimensional object; a collection of printed sheets; loudness

    The library has seven reference volumes dedicated to physics.

Vocabulary Practice with Word Forms

Read the following sentences. Circle the vocabulary word that best fits the sentences, in both definition and part of speech. Use your dictionary if necessary to identify any unfamiliar word forms.

1. If you were to choose (parallels / technology) between the ideas of two scientists, you might consider how Newton's ideas followed those of Galileo.

2. Students dealing with (stress / stressful) in their everyday lives must remain diligent in keeping up their grades.

3. Even with the (constraints / adjustments) of non-existent technology, early scientists managed to change the direction of physics.

4. When performing a physics experiment, it is crucial to (concentration / concentrate) on the exact procedures.

5. Dr. Jones' (technical / internal) skills are only surpassed by his intellectual skills.

6. We tried the experiment twice and got different results. This, we found out later, was because our objects weren't in (proportion / volume).

7. Students today can easily recreate theories of the past by using modern (parallels / technology).

8. (Adjust / Adjustments) had to be made to our calculations before they were officially written in our lab books.

9. Before sending off any scientific article to a publisher, it is important to get the results (proportionally / internally) verified.

10. To the naked eye, these two boxes are identical. Pick them up, however, and you will notice that the (volume / constraint) of the first box is much greater than the second one.

Discourse Markers

Study the following discourse markers and their functions. You will hear these discourse markers in the extended lecture.

Discourse Marker	Function
moving on	Shifting subtopics
pertains to	Showing a connection
to sum up	Summarizing / concluding

NOTE: For a complete list of discourse markers, see Appendix 2, page 129.

Listen and Respond

Consider Newton's First Law of Motion as you look at this picture.

ACTIVITY **9**

Listen to the Extended Lecture

First Listening: Listen for Discrete Vocabulary You will hear a lecture played two times. The first time, listen for words from the Academic Word List. Read the word pairs below. Put a check mark next to the word you hear. The words listed are in order in which they appear in the lecture.

1. _____ technique   _____ technical
2. _____ adjusted   _____ adjust
3. _____ parallelism   _____ parallels
4. _____ proportional   _____ proportion
5. _____ constraints   _____ constraining
6. _____ technological   _____ technology
7. _____ concentration   _____ concentrating
8. _____ stress   _____ stressful
9. _____ internal   _____ internally
10. _____ voluminous   _____ volumes

Second Listening: Listen and Take Notes Listen to the extended lecture again. Take notes using one of the methods you learned about in Chapter 1.

Compare your notes with those of a partner. Discuss any information that is different.

ACTIVITY ⑩   ***Answer Questions about the Extended Lecture***

Use your notes from the lecture to answer these questions. You may want to read the questions, then listen to the lecture again before answering.

1. According to the lecture, inertia is connected to
   a. acceleration
   b. Aristotle
   c. cars
   d. mass

2. According to the lecture, a push is an application of
   a. inertia
   b. mass
   c. acceleration
   d. force

3. Mass is used as a way to measure
   a. inertia
   b. speed
   c. force
   d. car accidents

4. Newton's first law of motion involves
   a. car accidents
   b. unbalanced force
   c. shift
   d. volume

5. You are looking in a parking lot, and you see many different types of vehicles. Based on the information in the lecture, which object below has the most inertia?
   a. a motorcycle
   b. a car
   c. a bus
   d. a scooter

6. In your own words, summarize Newton's First Law of Motion.

   _____

   _____

   _____

   _____

ACTIVITY ⑪   *Think Critically: Apply Newton's First Law*

In the lecture, you learned about Newton's First Law of Motion. Based on the information, it would seem logical that people are safer when using seat belts while traveling.

However, motorcycle manufacturers have not created motorcycles with seat belts. Are these manufacturers NOT safety conscious?

In groups of two or three, discuss the reasons for not using seat belts in motorcycles. Use some of the physics information presented in this chapter to explain your reasons.

ACTIVITY 12

Give a Group Presentation

Group presentations are commonly used by teachers in colleges and universities. The benefits are many, from allowing everyone to speak in a short format to sharing ideas and doing research together.

Task

You and your group of no more than three students will give a short presentation on Newton's First Law. Choose from one of the following examples to elaborate on or come up with your own. In your presentation use as many discourse markers and common phrases and expressions as you can.

- To get ketchup out of its bottle, the bottle is turned upside down, thrust downward at a high speed, and then stopped suddenly.

- When you put objects on a tablecloth (with most of the material over the side of the table) and pull the tablecloth, the objects do not fall off the table.

- In a car, a full cup of coffee tends to spill when you begin driving and when you stop.

- The head (top) of a hammer can be tightened onto the wooden handle by hitting the bottom of the handle against a hard surface.

- You can easily break a brick on someone's hand by slamming the brick with a hammer.

- Headrests are placed in cars to prevent injuries when a car hits you from behind.

- While riding a skateboard, you fly forward off the board when the wheel of the skateboard hits a rock.

Divide your presentation into three parts:
1. Introduction
2. Main point (describing the situation and why it occurs — how it shows Newton's First Law)
3. Conclusion

Guidelines
1. Decide on the topic of your presentation.
2. Choose one student to be responsible for each section of the presentation: introduction, body or main point, and conclusion.
3. Create at least one visual for the presentation. This can be a poster, photo, transparency, or something as simple as a graphic you put on the board. Just as in lectures, the more information you provide to your audience, the more they will learn.
4. Limit your presentation to 4 minutes.

Some Information about Group Presentations

Working together on a group project or presentation can be fun and instructive but has its pitfalls as well. One of the biggest complaints of group presentations is the lack of participation by all the members of the group equally. There is nothing more frustrating than working very hard to contribute to the group's progress only to find that one member of the group did not do his or her work. Most teachers do not take this excuse into consideration when grading an incomplete presentation, and the whole group may get a low grade.

For this reason, each member of the group must do the work assigned to him or her. If everyone shares the labor, the final product is sure to be complete and satisfying.

Organize the Presentation

While there is more than one way to organize a presentation, you can use the outline below to help you map out your ideas. See Appendix 6, page 141, for more information on presenting to a group.

SAMPLE OUTLINE

1. INTRODUCTION / Interesting hook:
   (Examples: Importance of physics, definitions, etc.)

   _____

   _____

   _____

   Main topic: _____

2. BODY / Explanation of the phenomenon and why it occurs:

3. CONCLUSION / Restate the main points, then give opinion, suggestion, or prediction:

Build a Rollercoaster

Practice some of Newton's Laws by building your own virtual rollercoaster. Just go to *elt.heinle.com/keyconcepts* and click on the link to Amusement Park Physics. Follow the directions for building a rollercoaster.

> For more activities and information, go to the *Key Concepts* 2 website at *elt.heinle.com/keyconcepts*.

Academic Word List Vocabulary[1]

Academic Word List word	Standard American Heritage phonetic spelling
academic	ăk´ ə **děm´** ĭk
access	**ăk´** sĕs
adequate	**ăd´** ĭ kwĭt
adjusted	ə **jŭst´** ĭd
alter	**ôl´** tər
alternative	ôl **tûr´** nə tĭv
annual	**an´** yo͞o əl
apparent	əp **păr´** ənt *or* ə **pâr´** ənt
approximate	ə **prŏk´** sə mĭt
attitude	**ăt´** ĭ to͞od´
attribute	ə **trĭb´** yo͞ot´ *or* **ăt´** rə byo͞ot´
circumstance	**sûr´** kəm stăns´
civil	**sĭv´** əl
code	kōd
comment	**kŏm´** ĕnt
commitment	kə **mĭt´** mənt
communication	kə myo͞o´ nĭ **kā´** shən
compensation	kŏm´ pən **sā´** shən
component	kəm **pō´** nənt
concentration	kŏn´ sən **trā´** shən
conference	**kŏn´** fər əns *or* **kŏn´** frəns
consent	kən **sĕnt´**
considerable	kən **sĭd´** ər ə bəl
constant	**kŏn´** stənt
constraint	kən **strānt´**
contrast	kən **trăst´** *or* **kŏn´** trăst´
contribution	kŏn´ trĭ **byo͞o´** shən

[1]Coxhead, Averil (2000)

convention	kən **věn´** shən
coordination	kō ôr´ dn **ā´** shən
core	kôr
corporate	**kôr´** pər ĭt *or* **kôr´** prĭt
correspond (with / to)	kôr´ ĭ **spŏnd´** *or* kŏr ĭ **spŏnd´**
criteria (pl)	krī **tîr´** ē ə
cycle	**sī´** kəl
debate	dĭ **bāt´**
deduction	dĭ **dŭk´** shən
demonstrate	**děm´** ən strāt´
dimension	dĭ **měn´** shən *or* dī **měn´** shən
document	**dŏk´** yə mənt
domestic	də **měs´** tĭk
dominant	**dom´** ə nənt
emerge	ĭ **mûrj´**
emphasis	**ěm´** fə sĭs
ensure	ěn **sho͞or´**
error	**ěr´** ər
ethnic	**ěth´** nĭk
exclude	ĭk **sklo͞od´**
framework	**frām´** wûrk
fund	fŭnd
goal	gōl
grant	grănt
hypothesis	hī **pŏth´** ĭ sĭs
illustrate	**ĭl´** ə strāt´ *or* ĭ **lŭs´** trāt´
immigration	ĭm´ ĭ **grā´** shən
implementation	ĭm´ plə mən **tā´** shən
implication	ĭm´ plĭ **kā´** shən
imply	ĭm **plī´**
impose	ĭm **pōz´**
initial	ĭ **nĭsh´** əl
integration	**ĭn** tĭ **grā´** shən
interaction	ĭn´ tər **ăk´** shən

internal	ĭn **tûr´** nəl
investigation	ĭn vĕs´ tĭ **gā´** shən
job	jŏb
justification	jŭs tə fĭ **kā´** shən
label	**lā´** bəl
layer	**lā´** ər
link	lĭngk
location	lō **kā´** shən
maximum	**măk´** sə məm
mechanism	**mĕk´** ə nĭz´ əm
minorities	mə **nôr´** ĭ tēz *or* mə **nŏr´** ĭ tēz
negative	**nĕg´** ə tĭv
obvious	**ob´** vē əs
occupational	ŏk´ yə **pā´** shən əl
option	**ŏp´** shən
outcome	**out´** kŭm´
output	**out´** pŏŏt´
overall	**o´** vər ôl
parallel	**păr´** ə lĕl´
parameter	pə **răm´** ĭ tər
partnership	**pärt´** nər shĭp
phase	fāz
philosophy	fĭ **lŏs´** ə fē
physical	**fĭz´** ĭ kəl
predict	prĭ **dĭkt´**
principal	**prĭn´** sə pəl
prior	**prī´** ər
professional	prə **fĕsh´** ə nəl
project	**prŏj´** ĕkt´ *or* prə **jĕkt´**
promote	prə **mōt´**
proportion	prə **pôr´** shən
publish	**pŭb´** lĭsh
reaction	rē **ăk´** shən
regime	rā **zhēm´** *or* rĭ **zhēm´**

register	**rĕg´** ĭ stər
reliance	rĭ **lī´** əns
remove	rĭ **mōōv´**
resolution	rĕz´ ə **lōō´** shən
retain (retention)	rĭ **tān´**
scheme	skēm
sequence	**sē´** kwəns
series	**sîr´** ēz
sex	sĕks
shift	shĭft
specify	**spec´** ə fī´
statistics	stə **tĭs´** tĭks
status	**stā´** təs *or* **stăt´** əs
stress	strĕs
subsequent	**sŭb´** sĭ kwĕnt´
sufficient	sə **fĭsh´** ənt
sum	sŭm
summary	**sûm´** ə rē
task	tăsk
technical	**tĕk´** nĭ kəl
technique	tĕk **nēk´**
technology	tĕk **nŏl´** ə jē
undertake	ŭn´ dər **tāk´**
validity	və **lĭd´** ĭ tē
volume	**vol´** yōōm *or* **vŏl´** yəm

Discourse Markers and Commonly Used Expressions[2]

The discourse markers are listed by function. Phrases in boldface appear in the chapters.

Introducing

In my talk today,

My topic today is

Today, we're going to discuss

Today, I'll go over

The purpose of my talk today is

Today we are going to look at

Giving Background Information

It is clear

It goes without saying

It is understood

As we know

As we have all read

Defining

X can be defined as

X is a type of Y

X is known as

X is actually

Just what is meant by

Listing

First,

To begin (with),

First and foremost,

Second,

Next,

The next point I'd like to cover

Another

Finally,

Showing a Connection

pertaining to

in connection with

Giving Examples

For example,

For instance,

X is a case in point.

Take X, for instance.

Take X, for example

Let me give you some specific examples:

The following are some common examples:

[2]Adapted from "Listening Comprehension and Note Taking." UEFAP. 9 Dec. 2002. *http://www.uefap.co.uk/listen/struct/liststru.htm*.

Emphasizing

The crucial point

We should bear in mind that

I want to stress

What's more,

In effect,

It is worth mentioning that

I'd like to emphasize

Fundamentally,

Furthermore

This goes to show that

Lest we forget,

It follows, then,

Clarifying

In other words,

Basically,

i.e.,

Let me put it another way.

In this respect,

That is to say,

If we put it another way,

What I mean to say is

Parenthetically speaking,

Shifting Subtopics

Now

OK

Now, I'd like to turn to

Moving on,

All right

Let's now look at

The next point I'd like to focus on

All that aside,

Giving Further Information

In addition,

Another point

Not only ... , but ...

On top of that,

Furthermore,

Moreover,

also

as well

Giving Contrasting Information

Although

On the other hand,

Despite

However,

Whereas

Nevertheless,

Giving an Opinion

As far as I'm concerned,

If it were up to me

If you ask me,

In my opinion,

According to

In my mind,

Classifying

There are X types/
   categories/varieties of

X can be divided into

Setting Parameters

In terms of

In the scope of

Digressing

By the way,   Before I forget,
Incidentally,

Concluding

We've seen that   In conclusion, I'd like to
In short,   To sum up,
Let me end by saying   Any questions?
All in all,

Commonly Used Expressions

Phrase	Definition
a point of contention	subject of disagreement
after all is said and done	after all debate is finished
all the more	even more
and so on	etcetera
at cross purposes	in contradiction to each other's intent
at the onset	at the beginning
back and forth	going and returning
foot the bill	pay all
get a grasp of	to understand
get the ball rolling	start
give rise to	cause
hardly the case	not the situation at all
in a fix	in a bad or difficult situation
in a nutshell	here is the basic point
instead of	rather than
it's all or nothing	completely or not at all
it's all very well and good	there is nothing wrong with … (but)
miss the point	not understand
no matter	it really isn't important
on the condition	if / depending on
owing to	due to
part and parcel of	a necessary and important element
poke holes in	find something wrong with
practically speaking	talking common sense
slowly but surely	done carefully over time
stem from	come from
supposing that	what if?
that isn't to say	it doesn't mean
the upshot of	the consequence or result
turning point	an important point of change in direction or meaning
when it comes down to it	the truth is
with the aim of	having the goal of
without regard to	ignoring
wrap up	finish
under no circumstances	not for any reason

Common Phrasal Verbs

NOTE: Phrasal verbs in boldface appear in the chapters.

ask out: ask someone to go on a date
be up to: busy with
bring out: reveal or show; make easier to see or experience; produce
bring up: rear (raise) children; mention or introduce a topic
call back: return a telephone call
call off: cancel
call on: ask to speak in class; visit
catch up with: reach the same level as someone or something
check in, check into: register at a hotel
check into: investigate
check out: take a book from the library; investigate
cheer up: make someone feel happier
clean up: make clean and orderly
come across: meet by chance
come up with: think of (an idea)
cross out: draw a line through
cut out: stop an annoying activity
do over: repeat, usually because it was not done correctly the first time
drop by: visit informally; leave something
drop off: leave something/someone at a place
drop out of: stop attending (a class, school, etc.)
figure out: find the answer by reasoning
fill out: complete a questionnaire or form by writing in the appropriate information
fill up: make something completely full or occupied
find out: discover information
get along with: have a good relation with
get away with: do something bad or mischievous and not get caught
get back (from): return from a place; receive again
get down to: begin; make a start
get over: recover from an illness or a bad experience
get through: conclude; finish
get up: arise from bed, a chair
give back: return an item to someone
give up: stop trying
go over: review or check carefully
go through: review or check carefully
hand in: submit an assignment

hang up: conclude a phone conversation; put clothes on a hanger or a hook

hold off: wait or delay

hold up: delay

keep out (of): not enter

keep up with: maintain the same level as someone or something

kick out (of): force someone to leave

leave out: omit; exclude

look after: watch over; guard; take care of

look back: re-examine; review

look into: investigate

look out for: be careful

look over: review or check carefully

look up: look for information in a reference book; try to locate a person

make do: manage; survive

make out: understand

make up: compose or form; invent; compensate for something

mean to: intend to do something

name after, name for: give a baby the name of someone else

nod off: fall asleep unintentionally

open up: initiate something; begin

pass away: die

pass out: distribute; lose consciousness

pick out: select

pick up: go to get someone; take in one's hand; learn

pile on: increase; strengthen

point out: call attention to; show

put away: move to a proper place

put back: return to original place

put off: postpone

put out: extinguish a cigarette or cigar

put up with: tolerate

read on: continue reading

run into, run across: meet by chance

run out (of): finish the supply of something

set off: begin; ignite

show up: appear, come

shut down: close

shut off: stop a machine, light, faucet, etc.

sit out: not participate or take part in something

split up: separate

talk out of: dissuade; convince someone not to do something

take advantage of: profit from; exploit

take after: resemble; look like

take for granted: not appreciate; undervalue

take over: take control

take up: begin a new activity or topic

tear down: demolish; reduce to nothing

tear up: tear into many little pieces

think over: consider carefully

throw away, throw out: discard; get rid of

track down: find

try on: put on clothing to see if it fits

turn down: decrease volume or intensity

turn in: submit an assignment; go to bed

turn off: stop the operation, activity, or flow of something

turn on: cause to begin operation or activity

turn out: arrive or assemble; result; extinguish a light

turn up: increase volume or intensity; find something that was missing

use up: use completely

work out: succeed

Word Forms of Words from the Academic Word List

NOTE: A word can take many forms in English, but only those forms with a strong connection in meaning are listed below.

Many verbs in English in their present and past participle forms can be used as adjectives. In the chart below, only those participial adjectives that are commonly found in speech and writing are included.

Noun	Verb	Adjective	Adverb
academics / academia	—	academic	academically
access	access	accessible / accessed	—
adequacy	—	adequate	adequately
adjustment	adjust	adjusted / adjustable	—
alteration	alter	altered	—
alternative	alternate	alternative	alternatively
—	—	annual	annually
—	—	apparent	apparently
approximation	approximate	approximate	approximately
attitude	—	attitudinal	attitudinally
attribute / attribution	attribute	attributive / attributed	—
circumstance	—	circumstantial	circumstantially
civility	—	civil	civilly
code	code / codify	coded	—
comment / commentary	comment	—	—
commitment	commit	committed	—
communication	communicate	—	—
compensation	compensate	—	—
component	—	componential	—
concentration	concentrate	concentrated	—
conference	confer	—	—
consent	consent	consensual	consensual
constant/constancy	—	constant	constantly

Noun	Verb	Adjective	Adverb
consideration	consider	considerable	considerably
constraint	constrain	constrain -ed/-ing	—
contrast	contrast	contrastive	contrastively
contribution	contribute	contribut -ed/-ing	—
convention	convene	conven -ed/-ing / conventional	—
coordination	coordinate	coordinat -ed/-ing	—
core	—	—	—
corporation	—	corporate	corporately
correspondence / correspondent	correspond	correspondent / corresponding	correspondingly
criteria	—	—	—
cycle	—	cyclic / cyclical	cyclically
debate	debate	debatable / debat -ed/-ing	—
deduction	deduct	deductible / deducted	—
demonstration	demonstrate	demonstrated / demonstrable	—
dimension	—	dimensional	dimensionally
document	document	documented	—
domestication	domesticate	domestic	domestically
dominance	dominate	dominant	dominantly
emergence	emerge	emergent / emerging	—
emphasis	emphasize	emphatic / emphasized	emphatically
—	ensure	—	—
error	err	erroneous	erroneously
ethnicity	—	ethnic	ethnically
exclusion	exclude	exclusionary / excluded	—
framework	—	—	—
fund	fund	funded	—
goal	—	—	—
grant	grant	granted	—
hypothesis	hypothesize	hypothetical	hypothetically
illustration	illustrate	illustrative / illustrated	illustratively
immigration	immigrate	—	—
implementation	implement	—	—

Key Concepts 2: Listening, Note Taking, and Speaking Across the Disciplines

Noun	Verb	Adjective	Adverb
implication	implicate / imply	implicated / implicit / implying / implied	implicitly
imposition	impose	imposing	imposingly
—	initiate	initial	initially
integration	integrate	integrated	—
interaction	interact	interactive	interactively
interior	—	internal	internally
investigation / investigator	investigate	investigative / investigat -ed/-ing	—
job	—	—	—
justification	justify	justifiable / justified	justifiably
layer	layer	layered	—
label	label	labeled	—
link	link	link -ed/-ing	—
location	locate	—	—
maximum	maximize	maximum / maximal	maximally
mechanism	mechanize	mechanical / mechanized	—
minority	—	—	—
negativity	—	negative	negatively
—	—	obvious	obviously
occupation	—	occupational	occupationally
option	—	optional	optionally
outcome	—	—	—
output	—	—	—
—	—	overall	overall
parameter	—	—	—
parallel	parallel	parallel	—
partnership / partner	—	—	—
phase	phase (in / out)	—	—
philosophy / philosopher	philosophize	philosophical	philosophically
—	—	physical	physically
prediction	predict	predictive / predictable / predicted	predictably
principal	—	principal	principally

Noun	Verb	Adjective	Adverb
—	—	prior	prior (to)
profession / professional	—	professional	professionally
project	—	—	—
promotion	promote	promoted	—
proportion	proportion	proportional / proportionate	proportionally
publication	publish	publish -ed/-ing	—
reaction	react	reactive	—
regime	—	regimented	—
registration	register	registered	—
resolution	resolve	resolute / resolved	resolutely
reliance	rely	reliant	reliantly
removal	remove	removed	—
retention	retain	retain -ed/-ing	—
scheme	scheme	scheming	—
sequence	sequence	sequential	sequentially
series	—	—	—
sex	—	sexual	sexually
shift	shift	shifting	—
specification / specifics	specify	specific / specified	specifically
statistics / statistician	—	statistical	statistically
status	—	—	—
stress	stress	stressful / stressed	stressfully
subsequence	—	subsequent	subsequently
sufficiency	suffice	sufficient	sufficiently
sum	sum	sum / summed	—
summary / summation	summarize	summarized	summarily
task	—	—	—
—	—	technical	technically
technique	—	—	—
technology	—	technological	technologically
undertaking	undertake	—	—
validity	validate	valid	validly
volume	—	voluminous	voluminously

APPENDIX 5 | Note-Taking Symbols

Many students like to use note-taking symbols during lectures. These types of symbols can save valuable time because they replace entire words or phrases with a shortened representation. However, because there is no one universal symbol for a particular word or phrase, symbols can be confusing.

You should not feel obligated to use symbols if you feel uncomfortable with them. If you are not used to the symbols or their verbal representation, you may make mistakes and use the wrong ones. Symbols should always be used in the same way. Use symbols only if you feel comfortable with them and know them well. If you need to spend a few seconds during a lecture trying to remember the symbol for something, you are defeating the purpose of saving time.

Common Note-Taking Symbols

Symbol	Meaning	Example
$=$	equals; is	Martin Luther King = activist.
$<$	less than	The population of the US is < 300 million.
$>$	more than	The average state income is > $25,000.
&	and	Smith & Jones developed the new formula.
w/	with	Biologists work w/ the scientific method.
w/o	without	He was arrested w/o warning.
$\uparrow$	increase	Military spending has ↑ recently.
$\downarrow$	decrease	Profits ↓ at Microsoft last year.
$\rightarrow$	causes	Smoking → cancer.
e.g.,	for example (Latin *exempli gratia*)	The troops needed supplies, e.g., weapons, vehicles, and more food rations.
i.e.,	that is; as in (Latin *id est*)	The leader was eliminated; i.e., he was assassinated.
$\cong$	approximately	The temperature is ≅ 76 degrees.
$\therefore$	therefore	Business is going well. ∴ stockholders will get better dividends.
#	number	The # of AIDS cases is rising.
aka	also known as	The plague, aka the "Black Death," spread throughout Europe.
%	percent	40% voted against the bill.
~	between	The current rate of inflation is ~1 & 2%.

Other Guidelines for Note Taking

1. Shorten dates: (July 4, 1776 = 7/4/76).

2. Use the first syllable and/or first few letters of the second syllable (history = hist).

3. Omit vowels (develop = dvlp).

4. Omit prepositions and articles (The Chancellor of Germany = Chancellor Germany).

5. After the first use, abbreviate proper nouns (Scholastic Aptitude Test = SAT).

Speaking in Class: Strategies for Presentations and Interactive Communication

Developing Confidence

Imagination Exercise

- Picture yourself in front of an audience.
- Watch yourself stepping out in front of the audience with confidence.
- Listen to the silence fall upon the room as you begin to speak.
- Feel the attention of the audience as you drive home point after point with confidence.
- Feel the warmth of the applause as you leave the platform.
- Hear the words of appreciation after your speech is over.

Helpful Tips

Seize every opportunity to practice speaking!

- Ask questions in class.
- Say hello to someone new every day.
- Join a club or an organization.

Develop confidence!

- Remember that you are not alone in your fear; more than 90 percent of the university population is afraid to speak in public.
- Some **stage fright** is useful! Adrenaline can make you think faster, speak more fluently and with greater intensity than normal.
- The *main cause* of your fear of public speaking is simply that you are not used to speaking in public!

Organizing Your Presentation

The Introduction

The introduction should contain a **hook** and the **main topic** that will be discussed (in that order).

The Hook

Fishermen use hooks to catch fish, and speakers use hooks to capture an audience. A hook should be an interesting

- quote
- statistic
- question
- anecdote (brief story)
- shared experience
- timeless truth

that is connected to your topic.

Example of a Hook

In a personal speech about a grandfather, the speaker uses this hook:

> "It was 1912, the same year that the Titanic sailed. But instead of traveling from England to New York, he went from Naples to Boston. The ship was crowded and dirty. Yet he survived the trip and countless other disasters. He was a man of great dignity. He was my grandfather."

Notice how the speaker did not begin the speech with, "Today I'm going to tell you about my grandfather." The audience is drawn in—hooked—by this little story of someone traveling on a ship to the United States. The speaker lets the audience know the main topic of the speech in the last sentence of the introduction: "He was my grandfather."

The Body

The body of a speech should be organized into main points with specific examples or supporting information. The audience should be able to pick out discourse markers and transitions to note shifts in the speech.

The Conclusion

The conclusion of an informational speech should contain two things:

1. a restatement or summary sentence
2. something that will leave your audience thinking about what you said

Here are a few examples of conclusions:

- a suggestion
- an opinion
- a prediction

Interactive Speaking: Asking and Answering Questions

When we listen to someone lecture, we sometimes want to ask questions to clarify a point or to get additional information. If someone is speaking and you want more information on the topic, there are good ways and bad ways to signal what you want. A bad way is to simply ask a question briskly: *What? Huh? What did you say? I didn't get that.*

Not only are these questions nonspecific, but to many people they sound rude. A better way to ask for additional or repeated information is to restate a part of what the speaker was talking about and then introduce your question. This method gives the speaker a frame of reference and invites a more relevant answer.

For example, note the differences between two types of questions. A speaker has just finished giving a presentation on the benefits of community colleges. A member of the audience asks: "John, where did you get your statistics?" While the information in the question is clear, the speaker might not know which statistics the audience member is referring to. A better way of phrasing the question is: "John, you just said something about the cost of community college studies. **My question is** … where did you get the statistics?"

When you give the speaker a frame of reference and signal that a question is going to come (in this case, *my question is* …), the speaker will listen more carefully to the question and be able to give a more specific answer.

Sample Evaluation Forms (Gradesheets) for Oral Presentations

I. Individual Presentations

Name of Speaker: _____

Speech Topic: _____

Date: _____

Content

Introduction

Creativity	6	5	4	3	2	1
Relevance to main topic	6	5	4	3	2	1

Transitions

Presence / use of transitions	6	5	4	3	2	1

Body

Organization of ideas / details	6	5	4	3	2	1

Conclusion

Summary of main areas	6	5	4	3	2	1

Content Score: _____ (max. 30 points)

Delivery

Eye contact	6	5	4	3	2	1
Confidence	6	5	4	3	2	1

Voice

Volume	6	5	4	3	2	1
Speed	6	5	4	3	2	1
Intonation	6	5	4	3	2	1

Delivery Score: _____ (max. 30 points)

Total Score: _____ (max. 60 points)

Comments:

II. Group Presentations

What Will Be Evaluated

Group Grade	**Individual Grade**
Information	Pronunciation
Completion	Clarity
Organization	Fluency
Presentation	Presence

Note: Group presentations will be timed.

Maximum time: _____ **minutes per speaker**
Going over the maximum time limit will result in a lower grade!

Names of Speakers: _____

_____

_____

_____

_____

Speech Topic: _____

Date: _____

Group Evaluation

Information / content	6	5	4	3	2	1
Completion	6	5	4	3	2	1
Organization	6	5	4	3	2	1
Presentation / delivery	6	5	4	3	2	1

Group Score: _____ (max. 24 points)

Individual Evaluation

Pronunciation	6	5	4	3	2	1
Clarity	6	5	4	3	2	1
Fluency (grammar / vocabulary accuracy)	6	5	4	3	2	1
Presence / delivery	6	5	4	3	2	1

Individual Score: _____ (max. 24 points)

Total Score: _____ (max. 48 points)

Comments:

III. Sample Student Feedback Forms

Basic Form

Basic Listening Task

Name of Speaker: _____

Date: _____

1. What is the main topic of the speech? _____

2. What was the purpose of the speech? _____

   _____

3. Write one specific detail from the speech. _____

   _____

Detailed Form

Speech Evaluation Form

Name of Speaker: _____

Speech Topic: _____

Date: _____

Content/Organization:

1. What was the hook or introduction of the presentation?

   question   anecdote   statistic   quotation   Other: _____

2. What was the main point of the presentation? _____

   _____

3. How did the presentation end?   *summary   suggestion   opinion   prediction*

Nonverbal Communication:
(Circle one)

4. Eye contact: excellent   very good   fair   needs work

5. Hand / body gestures: excellent   very good   fair   needs work

Verbal Communication:
(Circle one)

6. Pronunciation: excellent   very good   fair   needs work

7. Speed: excellent   very good   fair   needs work

Notes: _____

   _____

   _____
